RESISTANCE
TO
INNOVATION
IN
HIGHER
EDUCATION

By RICHARD I. EVANS

RESISTANCE TO INNOVATION IN HIGHER EDUCATION

CONVERSATIONS WITH CARL JUNG AND REACTIONS
FROM ERNEST JONES

DIALOGUE WITH ERICH FROMM

DIALOGUE WITH ERIK ERIKSON

Richard I. Evans
In collaboration with Peter K. Leppmann

Foreword by NEVITT SANFORD

RESISTANCE
TO
INNOVATION
IN
HIGHER
EDUCATION

A Social Psychological Exploration
Focused on Television and the Establishment

Jossey-Bass Publishers, Inc.
615 Montgomery Street · San Francisco · 1970

RESISTANCE TO INNOVATION IN HIGHER EDUCATION
*A Social Psychological Exploration Focused
on Television and the Establishment*
  by Richard I. Evans and Peter K. Leppmann

Jossey-Bass, Inc., Publishers
615 Montgomery Street
San Francisco, California 94111

Library of Congress Catalog Card Number 67-28627

Standard Book Number SBN 87589-010-5

Printed in the United States of America
by York Composition Company, Inc.
York, Pennsylvania

JACKET DESIGN BY WILLI BAUM, SAN FRANCISCO

FIRST EDITION
First printing: December 1967
Second printing: February 1970

671110

THE JOSSEY-BASS SERIES IN HIGHER EDUCATION

General Editors

JOSEPH AXELROD *and* MERVIN B. FREEDMAN

San Francisco State College

FOREWORD

In my course on the social psychology of higher education—which is based largely on studies of undergraduate students and which attempts to work out a theory of their development—we as a class come soon to share the view that the development of the individual student is the most important aim of undergraduate education and that there is much that colleges can do in furthering this aim. Then we come to the question: How can our various good suggestions for improving educational procedures be put into effect? How can colleges or universities—essentially conservative institutions—be induced to change? We consider faculty members, note that they have interest vested in things as they are, and suspect that they do not wish to change. We note, too, that the activities of individual teachers are interwoven with those of the institution as a whole and, hence, that even if a teacher wished to change nothing much would happen unless the institution itself was prepared to change. And as for the institution's changing, we are forced to recognize that our colleges and universities are embedded in the larger society, and that they rarely change according to their own plans but only in response to broad social forces.

Gloom begins to envelop the class, and notes of cynicism are heard. Students who have been planning to go into higher education with the thought that they might help to improve it begin thinking instead of how they might adapt themselves to the existing systems. Some members of the class point out, hopefully, that innovations *do* occur in our institutions of higher learning, that today in fact innovation is very much in the air. But others are quick to respond that innovations in established institutions are usually quite superficial, that for important improvements in undergraduate education we have to look to new or rapidly growing institutions, and that even here it is too early to tell whether new models are going to be sustained.

In my own efforts to relieve the bleakness of this picture, I have for the past several years pointed to the work of Richard Evans and his colleagues—work with which I had had some firsthand acquaintance. Perhaps, so I argued, we should restrain our pessimism about faculty attitudes until systematic and relevant studies of these attitudes were available; and surely we would not have long to wait, for the study of faculty members presented no unusual or insurmountable obstacles: All one had to do was begin by asking them about their work or about issues that concerned them as academic men or women—issues such as those posed by instructional television. More than that, we ought not to assume rigidity of faculty attitudes until we knew the results of serious attempts to change them.

It is thus a pleasure for me to see the work of Evans and his associates in print. It is especially gratifying to find in this book more than I had been led to hope for. We have here a wealth of data on teachers' educational philosophies and practices seen in relation to personality, background, and situation, the results of an experiment on attitude change in a real-life situation, a report on the use of television as a means for improving the work of the individual teacher. More than this, and probably most important, we have what the authors call a "research case history" of an innovation—the introduction of instructional television at "Metro University."

It has been a favorite dictum of mine that the thing to do about our colleges and universities is to study them, and that the best way to study them is to try to change them in some desired way, observing all the while the effects and the fate of one's efforts. The work described in *Resistance to Innovation in Higher Education* is a case in point. Evans and his colleagues were involved in an attempt to persuade the faculty of Metro University to consider the uses of instructional television. Here was something that most faculty members saw as having important implications—for good or ill—something that rapidly became controversial. Resistance was mobilized and lines of struggle were drawn, thus revealing much of the dynamic structure of the institution. In work of this kind the investigator is bound to turn up valuable information whether or not it was precisely what he had in mind. If the proposed innovation is appropriate and is adopted it will probably become a model for other institutions, and educational practice will thus be advanced; if the innovation is finally rejected the investigator will have learned something of institutional processes, something that will be useful in later attempts at change in the same or in different institutions.

In their case history, which was later supplemented by informal investigations at nine other colleges or universities, Evans and Leppmann were guided by sociological and social psychological theory pertaining to rigidity and change in social structures, and some of their findings would appear to hold for large organizations in general. The authors, however, are keenly aware of the limitations on the generalizability of their findings. They restrict their discussion to institutions of higher learning, and call for efforts to replicate and to extend their work in what they perceive as a broad and complex field of inquiry. They offer many suggestions concerning the directions that research ought now to take. So great is the need for knowledge of faculty attitudes and values and of the ways in which desirable innovations may be introduced in our colleges and universities that further studies of these topics are bound to be forthcoming soon. We may hope that they will build on this present one and that they will match it in methodological sophistication and orientation to theory.

Institute for the Study of Human Problems   *Nevitt Sanford*
Stanford University

PREFACE

With the current dramatic display of interest in the need for innovation in higher education on the part of government agencies, private foundations, and of higher education itself, traditional resistance to change in the American academic community has become increasingly more apparent and a greater focus of concern than ever before. Much speculation has been introduced concerning the nature of this resistance to innovation, but relatively little examination of this problem has been generated from the theoretical and research-based perspective of the behavioral sciences. *Resistance to Innovation in Higher Education* represents an exploration of the nature of resistance from such a perspective.

We recognize that the university as an innovation receiving system might profitably be regarded as any other institution in our culture to which innovations have been introduced. We introduce the problem of resistance to innovation in higher education by means of a concise summary of some of the various "models" in the literature that attempt to describe the diffusion of innovation that we feel may have relevance to innovation in the university.

We present a social psychological exploration of the role of the university faculty in the diffusion of innovation in universities. First, we review studies that have attempted to explore values, beliefs, and other personality characteristics of the university faculty and how they affect the process and function of innovation in higher educational institutions.

Then, in keeping with an increasing trend in social psychology to use "real life" settings to supplement the research that is effected in contrived, artificially controlled laboratory settings, a "research case history"—the course of an actual innovation in one "target" university—is utilized to serve as an example of the innovation process. It is based on attempts in this university to introduce, on a large scale, a widely considered innovation: the use of instructional television.

We relate in our research case history a study of the university faculty and innovation and social psychological theories of attitude change. On the basis of such theoretical formulations, a methodology is developed and implemented that allows us to evoke and analyze responses from the target university faculty.

We use two major approaches to expand the interpretation of the findings of the research case history, one primarily research based and the other theoretical. The research-based expansion of the data obtained from the research case history was prompted by an interest in determining, even in a limited way, the generalizability of the findings. Using specific questions suggested by the data from the research case history, we interviewed individual administrators and groups of faculty members from varying disciplines at a sample of nine other universities. The questions were designed partly to elicit an evaluation of the relevance of our findings to these other campuses.

In conclusion, we speculate concerning the possibilities for programming to deal with the problem of resistance to innovation in higher education.

We hope this book will provide encouragement to utilize further the university as a setting for behavioral research on the process of innovation. Such research cannot only contribute to the extension of important theoretical dimensions of the problem, but it should be of significant pragmatic value as well, since the success or failure in the diffusion of certain innovations will shape the entire future of the higher educational system.

Richard I. Evans

Houston, Texas   *Peter K. Leppmann*
October, 1967

CONTENTS

Contents

RESISTANCE
TO
INNOVATION
IN
HIGHER
EDUCATION

ONE

RESISTANCE TO INNOVATION IN HIGHER EDUCATION

One of the firm beliefs of our generation and of Western culture is that our age is one of unprecedented change in all areas of life—social and philosophical as well as technical. While we look on previous centuries and other cultures as backward and in some ways static, we point with equal pride and sophistication to the flexibility of our own society, which permits the rapid acceptance of almost any innovation with a minimum of social disorganization. However, when we subject this belief to a kind of Cartesian doubt and examine it without bias, we find that quite a different picture emerges. We realize that innovations were, and are, a part of every age and every culture and that—in every culture and every age, including our own—man is paradoxically confronted by the forces of innovation urging change, while, at the same time, he feels the impact of counter forces of folkways, mores, and other social controls which maintain stability.

Consider the age of Copernicus in the sixteenth century. Surely few innovations have had an effect as great as the heliocentric theory which this great mathematician and physicist proposed. Even though our own age—with its spaceships circling the earth and speeding toward the moon—views any geocentric theory as drastically out of date, we, nevertheless, realize that in the context of sixteenth century Europe, heliocentrism was considered an

1

innovation which a whole array of social forces opposed in the struggle to preserve the status quo as characterized by geocentrism.

Similarly in our day and culture, though innovations are springing up in unprecedented numbers, we can readily point to evidence that the conflict between the forces for change and those favoring permanence and stability is as real as ever. We need only to remind ourselves that the Scopes trial is part of the history of our culture and the present century. As recently as 1965, the textbook committee of a state legislature holding hearings on high school biology texts was confronted by an impressive group of literate citizens who bitterly opposed the teaching of evolution in the public schools. When we consider, furthermore, that in our research case history—which will be presented later—one of the respondents, a college professor, remarked that television is the "invention of the devil," we might indeed predict that Copernicus would have had as hard a time introducing some innovations to our generation as he did in his own time. Acceptance of an innovation in our age is far from universal. The speed of acceptance appears to depend not only on the innovation itself but on many other factors, including the nature of the social system and the character of its members.

Past investigations by behavioral scientists and others interested in the dynamics of change have shown that social institutions rarely include mechanisms for facilitating change. Definitions of social institutions most commonly stress their enduring and perpetuating aspects. Not surprisingly, then, the greatest resistance to change will be found in those institutions whose traditional, primary function has been the perpetuation of a society's folkways, mores, and values, such as religious and educational institutions. Paradoxically, the common assumption is that educational institutions, since they are charged with imparting both old and new knowledge to the young, must themselves be highly dynamic, with frequent changes in teaching methods as well as content. Furthermore, the assumption is that teachers and school administrators are such highly specialized experts in evaluating new developments in their field that from the many innovations offered they will carefully choose those which seem to provide the greatest potential for teaching.

Past studies of innovation in education have found little empirical evidence to support the above assumptions. In general, changes in educational methods have been exceedingly slow, due primarily to the climate of resistance and the educators' often outright hostility toward change. Among the most pessimistic findings on such change processes are those reported by Mort (1964), which indicate that some changes—such as physical examinations for school children—require more than a century from the time the need to innovate is recognized to the final diffusion of the innovation. C. P. Snow (1961), equally pessimistic about innovation in education, writes

> In a society like ours, academic patterns change more slowly than any others. In my lifetime, in England, they have crystallized rather than loosened. I used to think that it would be about as hard to change, say, the Oxford and Cambridge scholarship examination as to conduct a major revolution. I now believe that I was over-optimistic (p. 186).

Other investigators view the situation somewhat more hopefully. Miles (1964), for example, observes that comprehensive changes in the structure and functioning of American educational institutions are occurring now, that innovations of all sorts are being promoted and installed, but not always on their merits. Considerable evidence indicates that the nearly revolutionary changes in our educational system lack planning, integration, and, most of all, evaluation. Many changes are adopted only temporarily to be discarded later. This frequently results in a return to the old tried-and-true methods. The net change in innovations actually integrated into the educational process is small, and the tempo of the change process remains quite slow.

Higher education, as distinguished from primary and secondary education, can be characterized by even more traditional

3

patterns. Most of these traditions have their roots in the Renaissance, the period during which the European university systems were developed. To a considerable extent, the university community has been successful in resisting change, even though a dynamic and far more complex society has evolved around it. Such resistance to change has come, for the most part, from faculty members, who frequently emerge as champions for the preservation of the old institutional order. But the greatest threat to these traditional patterns comes from present-day society at large, whose perception of the university has undergone radical change.

Resistance to change may have both positive and negative aspects. Because this book focuses on innovation, it may sometimes give the impression that something is intrinsically good about change for its own sake. Change for change's sake—as we shall see later—could have detrimental effects on a system. Traditional values held in the field of higher education should not be suspect simply because in fact they are traditional. Educational institutions would indeed be derelict in their obligation to society if they were totally responsive to the fads and fashions of the surrounding community.

❧ INNOVATION IN THE UNIVERSITY ❧

Beginning with the development of the first universities in Europe 500 years ago and continuing into the early part of this century, the aura which surrounded institutions of higher learning and its professors was one of awe and mysticism. The populus at large saw the professor in various lights, perhaps as a great learned man, perhaps as someone who spoke in unintelligible tongues, or as an admirable person whose knowledge was "universal," or, often, even as one employed by evil forces to whom he had sold his soul in return for omniscience. The student saw his mentor as an idol, to be worshiped hopefully in exchange for some of the professor's vast knowledge. The general belief was that universal truth was finite, and upon completion of a prescribed course of study, the student would have absorbed all that his masters, the professors, knew and would then be ready to go into the world to find practical applications for his knowledge. In fact, many students remained at the university to become themselves the depository of knowledge that a new generation might tap.

This "universal" knowledge offered few, if any, pragmatic solutions to everyday problems. As a matter of fact, the isolation of the university was so complete and the ideas presented within its halls were considered so irrelevant to the surrounding community that political dictators—even demagogues—seldom saw the need to interfere with academic life. This was true even if the ideas presented were diametrically opposed to those of the dictator.

The contemporary university and its professors stand in stark contrast to their predecessors. Higher education has become everybody's business. In our day, the population looks to the university to provide solutions to a myriad of practical problems, ranging from the means for increasing agricultural production to more efficient methods of bookkeeping and better child-raising techniques. Without a doubt, this new role in which our society perceives institutions of higher learning, particularly the large urban or state university, has brought about drastic changes in some of the university's activities. The university and the community have been forced to interact. For one thing, the community—state or local or both—now wants not only to examine but frequently to control both what is being taught and the method of approach, insisting on measuring the effects of higher education with purely pragmatic criteria, usually a dollar-per-student yardstick. For another, the university community, or at least some of its members, is becoming increasingly aware that in an age when new facts accumulate with astronomic speed, the university can no longer hope to give the student a body of knowledge which will be adequate for the rest of his life.

With all the publicity focused in recent years on the population explosion in higher education, we need to say little here about the enormous changes which farsighted educators and laymen have predicted as a result of sheer numbers. Those who are informed about the problem are aware that unless the university prepares itself for this onslaught, educational quality will indeed deteriorate, with irreparable loss not only to the academic community but, even more important, to society in general.

If our everyday experience did not indicate otherwise, our knowledge of the dynamically changing role of the university would lead us to predict that the professor's role has also been drastically redefined, with resulting changes in his self-image that have profoundly influenced his value system. Moreover, we would assume that the newly emerged university, whose mammoth research programs have produced many of the new discoveries and applications of new principles, pioneers, whenever possible, the application of these new techniques to its own endeavors. But nothing can be further from the truth. Such a contradiction is not unlike that of the overweight physician who admonishes his patient to lose weight or risk a shortened lifespan. Eurich (1964) states the case very bluntly:

> The paradox is this: On the one hand we are vitally concerned with exploring the unknown, with challenging every old principle and with finding new knowledge in our fields of specialization. On the other hand we accept wholly the traditional methods or old wives' tales about teaching without any thought of improving our procedures (p. 51).

Obviously, if we want to resolve this paradox, we cannot just lament it or raise a didactic finger. To learn more about it, we should at least begin to institute research activity which might lead to its better understanding. As social psychologists we are interested in analyzing beliefs, values, and attitudes, and in experimentally developing methods and techniques for altering them. Thus we feel that social psychological research can help us understand the process of adhering to traditional values in the face of innovation. We realize that the college professor understandably dislikes to abandon tried-and-true methods of teaching in favor

6

of "experimentation" with innovations, since he feels that these will, at best, require his learning new techniques and, at worst, will threaten his very status and position. However, probing the many facets of this resistance to the change process seems to us to be in order.

The beliefs, attitudes, and values of the university faculty are the subject of a number of investigations and analyses, both subjective and objective. For example, Williams (1958) presents a subjective appraisal of the college faculty of one institution; Lazarsfeld and Thielens (1958) examine the effects of McCarthyism on academic freedom among a cross section of social-science faculty members selected from a sample of American colleges; Bowen (1960) in *The New Professors* presents an examination of university faculties in a series of essays by a group of individual professors; Russell's investigation (1962) in still another type of study focuses on faculty satisfactions and dissatisfactions at a specific university, those dealing with faculty morale; Sanford (1962) in *The American College* investigates in detail the unique kind of social institution which the American college represents and its relationship to the larger society; and Caplow and McGee (1958) in *The Academic Marketplace* examine the professor in the framework of the sociological and economic pattern in which he must function. However, none of these studies pursues the problem of faculty resistance to innovation through an objective, intensive investigation that is designed to produce empirical data based on a university faculty as a whole. Our research case history is designed to fill this apparent void.

❦ INSTRUCTIONAL TELEVISION ❦

We are primarily concerned about innovation in higher education in general. Who promotes change in higher education and where are the sources of resistance? Are some innovations more rapidly institutionalized than others, or can we be reasonably safe in making generalizations about all changes? These are the

7

basic questions which interest us. However, they are obviously far too global for us to answer empirically and objectively without first exploring more specific subquestions which may provide us with helpful data for finding answers to the larger questions. At the same time, a more definitive exploration does provide us with an opportunity to design and test useful instruments for further research of a more global nature.

Viewed within this context, our empirical study should be regarded as a "research case history" of innovation in higher education. It examines one academic community's response to a particular innovation, instructional television (ITV). However, along with assessing the degree of sympathy and antipathy that faculty members expressed toward this innovation in instructional media, the investigators also obtained data on their general beliefs and personality organization. Combining these more general data with specific attitudes toward ITV, the study introduces the reader to some prototypes of pro- and anti-ITV professors—prototypes who, although hypothetical, may provide valuable hypotheses about the innovator's and non-innovator's characteristics.

Finally, our research case history deals with the question of attitude change. Within social psychology a number of theoretical formulations concern attitude modification. Some of these we tested in a real-life setting experiment which, while free of the restrictions of a laboratory environment, did permit control of a number of variables.

Having thus moved from the broad issue of innovation in higher education to the more manageable study of faculty receptivity to ITV at one university, we felt that a return to the more general questions raised above would prove interesting. To gain some indication of how much we could generalize from the results of our research case history to other universities and innovations, we visited nine different schools to obtain some preliminary data. These university institutions varied in size and the source of their financial support and were located in the West, the Southwest, the

8

Northeast, and East.[1] In the interviews that we set up with a sample of their administrators and faculty members, we utilized a group of open-end questions to solicit their reactions to some of the principal findings of our research case history, as well as to gain some insight into their conception of innovations on their campuses in general. Drawn into a composite analysis, their replies and reactions appear in Chapter 8. Although this analysis is not derived from the systematically generated data of the kind we obtained in our research case history, we feel it has considerable value in providing the basis for identifying significant variables which future studies might examine further within the broader framework of the social psychology of innovation in the university, particularly in regard to the faculty's role in the change process.

In this respect, there have been a few reactions to a preliminary report (Evans, Smith, and Colville, 1963) of our study which suggest some misunderstanding of our intent. Some comments about these reactions may be appropriate at this point.

A few of the readers of the preliminary report apparently viewed it as a plea for abandoning traditional teaching methods in favor of instructional television. This emphatically is not our intention. We chose ITV as the focus of this study because it is a current and provocative example of an innovation in higher education. It also provided us with an unusual opportunity to explore variables influencing innovation.

At one end of the spectrum there are those who enthusiastically endorse ITV as the solution to all, or most, of the ills of American higher education; at the other end there are those who strongly oppose it and feel that it creates more problems than it will solve. We suggest, in less extreme terms, that ITV can be more properly perceived simply as a challenging departure from traditional teaching methods. As such, it represents an innovation

---

[1] We present a more detailed account of the methodology employed in this portion of our study in Chapter 8.

9

that should be objectively evaluated for its possible contribution to the university's teaching-learning system. It is an innovation which has aroused considerable interest among educators and laymen and has been introduced, at least experimentally, into a large number of educational institutions. Although ITV, like other innovations in higher education, is sometimes rejected for irrational reasons unrelated to its academic worth in the broadest sense, the contention that it or any other single innovation should be accepted as a panacea for American higher education is equally irrational.

A second, perhaps somewhat related, misinterpretation of our preliminary report is that the "heroes" of our study are the professors who favor ITV or similar innovations, while the professors opposed to ITV or similar innovations are the "villains." We did not intend to convey this impression. Unfortunately, such a result indicates that social psychological investigations which use "extreme groups" in an analysis are susceptible to misinterpretation. Indeed, our study does attribute various characteristics to the anti-ITV respondents which some people might consider undesirable. However, value judgments which one wishes to attach to such characteristics depend, of course, on one's own perspective regarding the proper role of professors in higher education. Thus, for example, some might well view the university orientation of our anti-ITV respondents as desirable, while others might view it quite differently.

We hope that we have identified some of the variables which may contribute to resistance to at least some innovations. We do not intend our study to reflect the belief that the personality characteristics of professors who resist innovation are necessarily less desirable than the traits of those involved in accepting innovation.

Finally, even though the focus of this book is innovation in American universities, we recognize that much attention is currently being paid to the problem of instituting change in universities in other parts of the world. The Agency for International Development (AID), for example, has begun to explore systematically

10

the problem of change in African, South American, and Asian universities. Some of the variables which we identify in our study might well be of interest to heads of programs directed at change in such institutions abroad. However, we believe that cross-cultural differences are, to say the least, crucial deterrents to the successful application of behavioral models from one culture to another. Furthermore, we feel that many of the early reports on innovations in foreign universities are too tentative and speculative to justify their incorporation within this book.

※ A CASE HISTORY ※

Any study which hopes to make a significant in-depth contribution to a given area of social psychology in a natural setting or field situation carries a high price tag. This is true both in respect to its financial requirements and the time and energy demanded from the investigators, the subjects, and the numerous other individuals who contribute their skills in such a major project. Hence, the investigators who undertake to study behavioral phenomena must employ methodologies and experimental designs which will provide data capable of the broadest possible interpretations and theoretical considerations without, of course, jeopardizing their applicability to the *specific* questions generic to the study.

Our investigation of faculty attitudes toward instructional television or ITV that we carried out at Metro University[2] is no exception to the above generalization. The primary phase of the project required a period of over two years and involved, in addition to the principal investigator, a sizeable research team, 319 subjects—of whom 108 contributed a considerable portion of their time for purposes of follow-up depth interviews—and, finally, 20

[2] The fictitious name "Metro University" is used to refer to the institution involved in the present study. There is, in fact, no university now in existence which reflects the *specific* characteristics ascribed to Metro University, because the actual institution has grown and developed so greatly in the few years since we gathered our original data.

11

subjects who as consultants devoted approximately 25 per cent of their time during one entire academic semester.

Because of the setting of the investigation and our belief that it may have significance within the broad framework of higher education, we propose in the present report to go beyond specific interpretations of our empirical findings, each of which can to some extent be considered as independent from the other. Some of these interpretations may provide valuable postulates related both to basic social psychological problems and to some rather practical problems concerning the process of innovation in the university. Others may point to the need for further investigations and/or contribute to the testing of existing theoretical frameworks.

In a sense, then, the reader will find that our presentation permits alternate levels of analysis, one or more of which may prove to be of particular interest to him. It may be helpful, therefore, to list some of the areas and approaches with which our study deals:

Instructional television. Certainly the exploration of existing attitudes toward, and future possibilities for, the use of television as an instructional device at the university level is a central focus. On this topic alone the data from our research case history may provide some social psychological perspective for those concerned with improving ITV as a useful tool for the college educator.

Higher education and the university. On a broader level, our research case history contains information about the urban university as an institution per se, particularly information about the personality structure of a faculty and its pattern of attitudes.

Attitude theory. Our data can be examined in the light of some of the prevalent social psychological theories about the formation and change of attitudes. An extended discussion of some of these theories and their relevance to our findings can be found in Chapter 5.

Methodology. We feel that our investigations may have value as an unusual model of social psychological research, particularly that aspect of it which is implemented in a natural behavioral or field setting. Because of the many difficulties involved in studying behavior in "the everyday world," much testing of social psychological theory has been conducted in more or less contrived laboratory settings. As a result, questions often arise concerning the generalization of research findings, since such experimental situations often are too removed from natural behavioral or field situations. Evans (1966b), as well as other social psychologists such as Sanford (1965) and Sherif (1961), have recently attempted to make a case for the importance of natural field-setting research dealing with significant human problems. In this respect, our investigation represents an unusual departure from many previous investigations concerned with testing hypotheses implicit in social psychological theory.

Innovation theory. A broader theoretical model than is usual in the traditional studies of attitude change in social psychology is emerging from work based upon the study of behavior patterns in various natural social settings. It is perhaps premature to construct viable theories from this model, since extrapolations from such studies are often tenuous and the rapidly accumulating studies do not necessarily relate systematically enough to develop authentic theories in the most sophisticated sense. However, we feel that the possibility of developing these may be at hand and that the present study may make a contribution toward this end. In order to begin to project such hypotheses and as a mechanism for developing ones useful to our own study of innovation in higher education, we will attempt in the next chapter to present and analyze some of the more provocative theories. Some of these are entirely speculative; some are more solidly based on empirical work. From them we hope to highlight significant variables which must be involved in the examination of innovation in educational settings.

TWO

THEORIES OF INNOVATION

What factors contribute to the prompt diffusion and rapid adoption of one particular innovation, while another—introduced at the same time into the same social system—is rejected or requires far greater time for its adoption? This question underlies many of the studies on diffusion of innovation.

Most investigations into the diffusion of innovation have been approached in the context of those behavioral sciences which are concerned primarily with collective rather than individual behavior and thus place proportionately greater emphasis on the nature of the social system than on the individual. Rogers (1962), for example, lists the following six major diffusion traditions: (1) anthropology, (2) early sociology, (3) rural sociology, (4) education, (5) industrial sociology, and (6) medical sociology. However, he points out that every area of the behavioral sciences has some interest in diffusion of ideas. We might expect, then, that social psychology, whose prime interest is individual behavior within the social environment, would be a fertile field for the study of the diffusion of innovation.

Many models of innovation research have emerged from the above traditions, some rather vague and ill defined, a few carefully worked out and precisely defined. Among this latter group are the formulations by Katz and Levin (1959) and by Katz (1961) alone. These investigators pinpoint four crucial elements in the analysis of the diffusion of an innovation: (1) the tracing of an innovation, (2) over time, (3) through specific channels of communication, and (4) within a social structure. To these we might add a fifth element, that is, the individuals or groups within the social system which are in a personal way confronted with, sometimes even threatened by, the innovation.

With this addition, our investigation meets the criteria that Katz outlined in 1961. In our research case history concerning innovation in universities, we are essentially investigating the diffusion of instructional television (ITV), by individuals or groups (faculty members and the various departments), over time, linked to specific channels of communication (for example, the original letter from the investigators through the Dean of Faculties to the entire Metro University), within the social structure of the university community.

It appears, then, that four major components influence the process whereby an individual or a group becomes aware of, evaluates, and finally accepts or rejects an innovation. To begin with, there is the innovation itself, which means a new idea or a new cultural object—even in the latter case, however, it is the idea about the object which is diffused. Second, there is the process itself, beginning with the introduction either from within or from without the social system, its promotion, and final adoption. Third, there are the characteristics of the individuals or groups which make up the membership of the social system, and, fourth, there is the nature of the social system itself, the context into which the innovation must be incorporated. The system can be a society or merely a subgroup, such as the university faculty in our study.

❧ CHARACTERISTICS OF INNOVATION ❧

As used in the studies we have mentioned, an innovation seems to have two subcomponents. First, there is the idea or item

15

which is novel to a particular individual or group and, second, there is the change which results from the adoption of the object or idea. We would also include among innovations those items or ideas which represent a recombination of previously accepted ideas. For example, in our research case history, television can be considered an innovation which has been broadly accepted but whose use as a teaching device has encountered strong resistance.

Evidence also indicates that we should discard from the start any notion that the speed with which an innovation is adopted is necessarily related to its usefulness to society as a whole. For example, the glue-sniffing fad among teen-agers has been rapidly diffused throughout the country but can hardly be considered beneficial to our society. In a more basic vein, the reluctance of many Americans to accept fluoridation of water supplies for the prevention of tooth decay (Evans, 1965; Gamson and Lindberg, 1960) can hardly serve as an objective criterion for evaluating the effectiveness of fluorides. As a matter of fact, Miles (1964) goes so far as to say that "educational innovations are almost never installed on their merits" (p. 635). The value, then, of an innovation to society does not provide us with a criterion for predicting the speed with which it will be accepted or rejected.

The findings of our investigation support the view expressed by Rogers that the actual characteristics of an innovation are of little importance to its adoption. What does seem to matter is the way in which the individual perceives the relative values of an innovation. For example, the data from our research case history indicate that the "innovators" (pro-ITV) actually did perceive ITV differently from the "laggards" (anti-ITV). Attempts, then, to delineate the different characteristics of an innovation might very well proceed from the perceptions of the individual or the group—that is, they would make subjective rather than objective evaluations. Rogers lists five characteristics which, when viewed from the standpoint of individual or group perceptions, past research has found to affect the rate of adoption: (1) relative advantage, (2)

16

compatibility, (3) complexity, (4) divisibility, and (5) communicability.

The individual confronted with an innovation will determine its relative advantage largely on the basis of whether he thinks it superior to the ideas which it supersedes. Thus, we were aware that the professors at Metro would have to perceive ITV as essentially superior to traditional teaching methods if this factor was to affect the rate of its adoption. Although economic advantage is also listed under this category, other advantages such as reduced teaching load and more time for research may be included here, too.

Compatibility of an innovation concerns the degree to which potential adopters feel it is consistent with their existing values and past experiences. This characteristic appeared to contribute heavily to the slow rate of adoption of ITV. Most of our respondents saw the innovation as wholly inconsistent with the university climate as they perceived it. To them ITV either lacked or failed to contribute to the important ingredients of personal contact between teachers and students, feedback from students, and proper supervision of students, all of which they considered essential to the learning process.[1]

Our respondents' recognition that ITV would require special training, would expose weaknesses in teaching methods, and would lend itself to the teaching of only certain subjects indicates the degree of complexity with which they viewed the innovation.

Not all innovations, of course, require full acceptance or complete rejection. Most, if not all, can be perceived as divisible into stages which may make adoption less painful. The most frequent divisibility that potential adopters employ is that of limited adoption, which by not requiring wholehearted acceptance of an innovation leaves the way open to return to an older idea at any time. This phenomenon appears to be the case with ITV, as we

[1] See Appendix 3 for a comparative analysis of the reasons that faculty members gave for accepting and rejecting ITV at four universities.

17

will indicate later, and emerges with such regularity from the histories of ITV diffusion on the American campus that we feel we can identify it with the term "reversion effect."

A kind of pseudo acceptance of an innovation results—for example, acceptance of ITV on a limited basis. The administrators and/or faculty members involved announce that it is "adopted experimentally," which makes later abandonment—and reversion to older processes—so easy that it is almost inevitable. This "experimental" phase can last for extended periods of time, often years, postponing rejection or complete adoption almost indefinitely. The immediate cause of the reversion may under these circumstances be quite insignificant in long-range terms, such as the temporary breakdown of equipment, the lack of properly trained personnel, or the curtailing of budgetary allocations. For example, under the heading of maintaining ties with earlier practices—which also contributes to setting the stage for reversion—our respondents generally found the combination of ITV with more traditional education methods, such as discussion sessions and laboratory periods, more acceptable than straight television courses. This was the case even when they found it difficult to show how this combination contributed significantly to student learning.

Finally, rate of adoption is a function of the degree to which the effects of an innovation can be communicated to others. This is, of course, a two-way street; both negative and positive effects can be communicated. Again, we are dealing here with perceived rather than actual results. Thus, we found a prevailing belief among faculty members that students enrolled in television courses necessarily learn less than those enrolled in traditionally taught courses. Actually, a wide variety of studies have shown no significant differences in learning performance between television and non-television courses.

One further broad distinction must be made between types of innovations. Some innovations by their very nature require acceptance or rejection by the total social system with relatively little freedom of choice for the individual member, while others permit

18

him to accept or reject an innovation independent of the group action. We will return to this aspect of the problem in our discussion of the system itself; however, the distinction between these two categories of innovations is in itself important. For example, although a member of a community can decide independently whether or not to acquire a television set, he would find it more difficult to reject fluoridation which has been adopted by a community whose water supply he shares.

Innovations vary greatly in the amount of change which their adoption brings to a given social system, and this may directly influence the speed of diffusion and adoption. Miles (1964) alludes to this possibility when he states that "other things being equal, innovations which are perceived as threats to existing practice rather than mere additions to it are less likely of acceptance; more generally innovations which can be added to an existing program without seriously disturbing other parts of it are likely to be adopted" (p. 638).

❧ INNOVATORS AND LAGGARDS ❧

Our study at Metro, among other things, attempts to ferret out the personality characteristics of those individuals who displayed certain identifiable attitudes toward instructional television. A useful method for this purpose is the psychological analysis of extreme or diametrically opposed groups which we will discuss in Chapter 6. Although this method of analysis is common to many studies in the behavioral sciences, it is frequently accompanied by the danger of overinterpretation or even misinterpretation. As suggested earlier, some professors who read a preliminary report of our research case history (Evans, Smith, and Colville, 1963) reflected such an incorrect interpretation. Because these readers were opposed to ITV, they thought they were being portrayed as necessarily possessing *all* of the traits attributed to the hypothetical anti-ITV group. Apparently viewing these traits as undesirable, they often reacted to our findings defensively. We must repeat, then, that the presentation of characteristics of such atypical groups is primarily valuable because it permits the researcher to make general comparisons which may yield fruitful hypotheses for future research. Investigators using this device do not necessarily imply the actual existence of individuals or groups who possess all or even most of these characteristics. Such prototypes are, in fact, pure abstractions of the sample of behavior under analysis. For example, it is statistically possible for an individual to favor or oppose ITV and not actually possess any of the characteristics found among the extreme pro- or anti-ITV groups.

Rogers characterizes five adopter categories as "ideal" types; again, these are abstractions that apply to prototypes of the kind described above, although he apparently did not deduce them from research data like those produced in our ITV study. However, each of his categories is also characterized by particular attributes.

For purposes of our present investigation, we are concerned primarily with the two prototypes emerging from our research case history. Because Rogers' speculations concerning different types of innovators appear to provide an interesting framework within which our research findings can be presented, we shall use it in our later discussion. His five adopter categories along with the salient values he attributes to each are (1) innovators—venturesome—willing to accept risks; (2) early adopters—respected—regarded by many others in the social system as model; (3) early majority—deliberate—willing to consider innovations only after peers have adopted them; (4) late majority—skeptical—overwhelming pressure from peers needed before adoption occurs; and (5) laggards—tradition bound—oriented to the past.

On the basis of a number of studies, Rogers concludes that plotting these adopter categories over time yields close to normal distributions which may be used to delimit the five categories. Thus, early-majority adopters fall within the 34 per cent representing one standard deviation below the mean, while late-majority adopters are one standard deviation above the mean. Laggards

20

make up the 16 per cent of the upper tail of the curve, while the lower tail shows early adopters comprising the 13½ per cent above the first standard deviation. Finally, the 2½ per cent above the second standard deviation are labeled as "innovators."

The innovator or innovating group has the task of introducing an innovation into a social system and guiding it along a frequently circuitous route to adoption. As we have stated, an idea can come from a source external to, or part of, the innovation-receiving system. It can be introduced by a "change agent," a term that Rogers and others use to identify a professional person who tries to influence the direction that decisions on adoption will take. This permits the distinction between one who simply introduces change and the innovator who is really the first person within the system to adopt an innovation. The change agent has emerged as an important figure in many areas of innovation research; he is the county agent in agriculture and the drug-detail man in medicine. In the field of education, however, such change agents are virtually non-existent. This lack may be one reason why so many members of an educational system are frequently uninformed about changes in content and technique in their particular area of teaching. The book salesman, for example, cannot be classified as a change agent, since his main purpose is not to change but simply to continue the long-standing method of promoting certain textbooks. The responsibility for introducing an innovation into a university usually falls, then, to the person who is also the first adopter. We will therefore use the term "innovator" to mean a person, or a group, who introduces a new idea, as well as the one who is first to adopt it.

Who is the innovator? What personality characteristics does he share with other innovators? What are his values, his reference groups, and his attitudes? What is the hierarchy of his loyalties? A composite picture of the innovator, admittedly set forth as an "ideal type," is presented by Rogers (1962):

Observers have noted that venturesomeness is almost an obsession with innovators. They are eager to try new ideas. This interest leads them out of a local circle of peers and into more cosmopolite social relationships. Communication patterns and friendships among a clique of innovators are common even though the geographical distance between the innovators may be great. They travel in a circle of venturesomeness, like circuit riders who spread new ideas as their gospel. Being an innovator has several prerequisites. They include control of substantial financial resources to absorb the loss of an unprofitable innovation and the ability to understand and apply complex technical knowledge. The major value of the innovator is venturesomeness. He must desire the hazardous, the rash, the daring and the risking (p. 169).

Like the rugged pioneer of nineteenth-century America, who really was an innovator himself, the innovator possesses some character traits that do not appear to be socially desirable. As a matter of fact, almost by definition, other members of the social system perceive him as deviant to some degree. Rogers points out that the degree to which innovators are perceived as deviants depends in part on the social system's norms for what constitutes innovation. Hence, in a social system which is generally more tradition oriented, as most university communities are, the innovator is perceived as highly deviant. He will likely consider himself to be a deviant, too, though if he does he will identify with reference groups outside the system who validate his behavior and, thus, to use Rogers' paraphrase of Thoreau, he will "find himself in step with a different drummer."

That the motives for advocating or supporting change are not always identical or necessarily clear is suggested by Barnett's interesting typology of innovators (1953):

1. *The Dissident:*
   who have "consistently refused to identify themselves with some of the conventions of their group."
2. *The Indifferent:*
   who are prepared to accept new ideas because they have not

22

dedicated themselves irretrievably to a custom or an ideal of their society.

3. *The Disaffected:*

   who are at odds with their society as a result of such possible variables as marginal status, disillusionment, frustration, circumvention by specified enemies, generalized social anxiety, guilt depression.

4. *The Resentful:*

   who are susceptible to a suggestion of change because they have less to lose by accepting it, often nothing to lose (p. 381).

The diversity of motives, often occurring even within one individual, may explain some of the puzzling results of our study with regard to the pro-ITV professor. An innovation may appeal to a particular individual purely because he has become disenchanted with the old order. Watson (1964) in his study of an innovation in education describes such a group of "pseudo innovators," as we might label them. Although they are dissatisfied with traditional ideas, sooner or later their emotional or personality problems lead to equal dissatisfaction with the innovation. In their first enthusiasm, members of such a group are often unrealistic about their expectations and soon become disillusioned and resentful. They then repeat their pattern of rebellion. Actually, they are not real innovators, for if diffusion depended on them, no innovation could flourish. To be successful, the innovator must maintain a delicate balance between deviance and conformity.

The requirements for a successful innovator are pinpointed by Clee and Reswick (1964): "In designing and implementing educational innovations hard work, patience and courage are required to overcome fantasies and stereotypes so that trust can be built and help given and accepted as common objectives are faced" (p. 81). Tarde (1903), one of the early advocates of modern sociological analysis, sets forth the requirements for innovators in this manner: "To innovate, to discover, to awake for an instant the individual must escape for the time being from his social sur-

23

roundings. Such unusual audacity makes him super social rather than social" (p. 87). Perhaps one of the most vivid anecdotal descriptions of an innovator is that of Thomas Alexander by Watson (1964): "He was a creative maverick who wore no educational or political brand. He was an individualist with little confidence in collective decisions. He was basically kind and fair minded, but he rather enjoyed shocking people with unexpected and extreme pronouncements. His bark was worse than his bite" (p. 100).

One interesting paradox emerges when we rate the innovator on a practical-theoretical scale. We intuitively assume that researchers, inventors, and teachers are surely innovators. This appears not to be the case. Miller (1957) states that "Typically, the innovators were practitioners who were involved in research and academic teaching as a sideline" (p. 23). Our own findings would support this view. The innovators (pro-ITV professors) came generally from the more pragmatic areas of the university, and were removed from the more academic core. Furthermore, their focus tended to be away from the academic endeavors of the university, particularly classroom teaching. In general, the innovator also appears to be favored with relative financial security. Thus Ross (1958), reviewing a number of studies dealing with educational innovation in public schools, concludes that the one variable most closely related to the ability to innovate is the relative financial security of the innovator. The question that Ross raises in regard to cause and effect is, of course, quite legitimate: Are innovators economically secure because they innovate or do they innovate because they are economically secure? In our study we detected some tendency for a positive attitude toward ITV to be related to a respondent's better financial position, though such evidence was indirect.

On the other end of the spectrum of adopter categories is the laggard. He is the last in a social system to adopt an innovation, if it is adopted at all. Rogers points out that such an individual must be considered as deviant as the innovator. While the latter underconforms to the standards of his society, the former overconforms to traditional values and ideas. Predictably, many studies, including our research case history, have found the laggard's salient values to be oriented toward the traditions of the past. In most systems the laggard shares with his opposite, the innovator, a low social status. High social status and respect tend to be bestowed upon the more moderate adopter, and in the adopter-laggard scale fall near its center at a point slightly favoring innovations. Past research also indicates that the laggard does not tend to specialize in his field, generally plays a small role in the social system, and is frequently older that his innovator colleague. This might lead us to speculate that all these characteristics indicate the laggard's position in society is rather insecure. As a matter of fact, Rogers (1962) confirms this hunch from his analysis of several studies, stating that "laggards are most likely to drop out of the social system" (p. 192).

As we pointed out earlier, an innovator needs a cosmopolite orientation, that is, one which is external to a particular system. The laggard avoids such orientation; as a result, his horizon is limited and his information sources are confined to a narrow environment. Neighbors, friends, and relatives with values similar to his own are his main source of information. Actually the extreme laggard could be described as an isolate or at least a semi-isolate.

Again, our study supports some of these hypotheses, which we have taken for the most part from Rogers' review. We will present our data related to this conception of cosmopolite and localite professors in Chapter 6. These data indicate the tendency for extremely anti-ITV professors to identify with traditional values in the system. Their preoccupation with traditional methods of classroom teaching, student evaluation, and a generally less cosmopolite orientation endows them with some of the characteristics which predict non-innovative behavior.

Summarizing the attributes of the laggard, we again quote Rogers (1962) in describing this "ideal type":

Laggards are the last to adopt an innovation. They possess almost no opinion leadership. Laggards are the most localite of all adopter categories, and many are near-isolates. The point of reference for the laggard is the past. Decisions are usually made in terms of what has been done in previous generations. The individual interacts primarily with others who have traditional values. When laggards finally adopt an innovation, it may already be superseded by another more recent idea which the innovators are using. Laggards tend to be frankly suspicious of innovations, innovators and change agents. Their advanced age and tradition direction slows the adoption process to a crawl. Adoption lags far behind awareness of the idea. Alienation from a too-fast-moving world is apparent in much of the laggard's outlook. While most individuals in a social system are looking for the road to change ahead, the laggard has his attention fixed on the rear-view mirror (p. 171).

Are innovators or laggards consistent in their behavior? As is the case with most human behavior, the evidence would tend to indicate considerable inconsistencies. Although Rogers reports some evidence that innovators consistently adopt innovations in a given category, for example, new methods of livestock feeding or crop rotation, in other areas there appears to be less certainty. Thus, a farm innovator may not be an innovator in such areas as political ideology, consumer behavior, or education. Our own data seriously challenge any consistency hypothesis. The results of our factor analysis, discussed briefly in Chapter 5 and reported more completely in Appendix 2, indicate that attitudes which suggest non-innovative or lagging behavior toward ITV may stand in relative isolation from attitudes toward other objects in the individual's environment. Furthermore, our analysis of the prototypes of the pro- and anti-ITV professor also points to such inconsistencies. Whatever the reasons may be for these, we found that the extremely anti-ITV professor favored such perceived innovations at his university as state support for his school and the admission of qualified Negroes, while the extremely pro-ITV professors were less favorably disposed toward them. But how predictable these behavioral inconsistencies are is, of course, a matter of conjecture.

❦ SOCIAL SYSTEM OF THE INNOVATOR ❦

Adopters, whether innovators, laggards, or in-between, live in social systems within which the diffusion of an innovation must take place. This innovation-receiving system (Miles calls it the "target system") is simply comprised of individuals who are engaged in endeavors with similar or identical goals. Such a system may be clearly specified, for example, a particular school district or university faculty; or it may be less clearly defined in the sense of referring to all farms in a particular county or state.

Many students of social systems, as they study the diffusion of innovations, have placed major emphasis on the social system itself. Social psychologists—looking at such problems from the individual rather than institutional level of analysis—tend to place greater emphasis on the individual's role within the social system and the way he affects and is affected by it. Nevertheless, we do not mean to imply that psychologists do not consider the nature of the social system as tremendously important to any change process. We must remember that the system was pre-existent to, and will continue to exist after, the innovation has been diffused. Generally, the basic values and characteristics of the social system also existed prior to the time a particular individual became a member of it. This would be an argument in favor of analyzing the system apart from the individual member. Yet we know, of course, that the social system, at least to some extent, governs and is governed by the individual's behavior; thus we would find it difficult to discuss the system without reference to its members' characteristics.

Some of our preliminary inferences regarding the consistency of certain faculty responses at all ten of the universities with which our report deals make us suspect that the manner in which a system influences an individual member's judgment of an innova-

27

tion could be subjected to analysis within the framework of the Adaptation Level Theory. Advanced originally by Helson (1947), this theoretical model provides mathematical formulations which permit quantitative predictions concerning an individual's changing judgment of physical stimuli, such as size, weight, and loudness; these predictions are based not only on the characteristics of the stimulus to be judged but also on previous experience with similar stimuli and the background or context within which the particular stimulus is to be judged. Helson found evidence that these factors combine to form a neutral point or adaptation level against which new stimuli would be judged. Further judgments, however, would cause the adaptation level to shift in a predictable direction and amount.

Several investigators have found that the usefulness of this model is not limited to the study of sensory perception but may, in fact, be utilized for studying a wide variety of psychological phenomena, including social judgments. Thus, experimental evidence indicates that ratings of skin color or the physical heights of others can be quite independent of the subjects rated and even depend to a significant extent on the rater's past experience (Marks, 1943; Philip, 1951). In another study along the same line, Hinckley and Rethlingshafer (1951) conclude that judgment of the melodiousness of Shakespearean poetry is influenced by the background against which it is presented. Their raters' judgments were enhanced by knowledge of the poet's name, while knowledge of the literary period without specific identification of the poet lowered their opinion of the perceived melody. Asch (1952) and Sherif (1935), among others, also suggest that in understanding and predicting social behavior, descriptions of even complex social stimuli in themselves are less important than the knowledge of how the individual views them within his subjective context.

Applying the concept of adaptation level to the study of innovation—particularly to that in higher education—we would postulate that an individual's judgment of the value of a particular novel idea would be considerably influenced by his own past ex-

28

perience with similar innovations and by the general climate of the university—for example, whether it encourages or discourages change. Furthermore, we would postulate that these factors could operate quite apart from the specific innovation itself.

Past research does indicate that we can make some predictions about the rate of diffusion of an innovation based on the general characteristics of a social system's norms. Rogers provides such generalizations, again in the form of prototypes. He projects the prototype norms of a system as being either traditional or modern. The traditional system is characterized as having a less developed technology than the latter and little communication by its members with those outside it. Most individuals in the system are localites rather than cosmopolites. They lack the ability to empathize or see themselves in the role of another person, particularly someone outside the system. Members are also slow to recognize new roles or to learn easily new social relationships involving themselves. In this system, precedent outweighs all other guidelines to behavior, a phenomenon which Weber (1958) calls the "authority of an eternal yesterday" (p. 78).

In contrast, Rogers presents the typical modern social system as one which is technologically advanced with a complex division of labor. Members are generally more urbane and more cosmopolite in their relationships than those in a traditional system. New ideas can enter more freely from the outside, partly because members frequently interact with others outside the system. Careful economic planning and the use of the most effective means to achieve desired ends are also part of the modern orientation. Furthermore, individual members within the modern system are better able to see themselves in the role of others.

No one, however, should unconditionally assume that such social structures actually exist with all or even most of the above characteristics. The rate of diffusion of an innovation is, in fact, dependent on a number of elements, no single one of which can be used as a sole predictor. Ample evidence from the studies on innovation show that a particular system can have a traditional

29

orientation, generally rejecting or retarding change, yet provide a favorable climate for the rapid diffusion of a particular innovation. Similarly, rejection or retardation of a particular innovation by a modern system may also occur.

The values and characteristics of either social system do, of course, play a significant part in the way the adopter of an innovation perceives his role, as well as the way in which his role, in turn, is perceived by others. Stated more simply, an individual's orientation is strongly related to the orientation of a particular system. A system with a high degree of traditional orientation is likely to regard our prototype the laggard as an opinion leader, while viewing the innovator as highly deviant and marginal to its social processes. In contrast, the progressive society, oriented more to the contemporary scene, often looks to the innovator for leadership, while rejecting any attempt on the part of the laggard to exert his influence. Systems which have an orientation somewhere between these two extremes cast both the innovator and the laggard in the role of deviant, while probably looking toward the moderate elements for leadership. A contemporary example is the development of the civil rights movement in the South. Apparently, more often than not, the community looks to some of its more moderate members to supply the crucial leadership to the movement in which innovation was a major component.

Past studies indicate that differences between individuals in the ability to innovate seem to inhibit the flow of influence in the modern system, thereby preventing or, at least, discouraging communication between innovator and laggard. In the traditional setting, however, laggards might actually seek certain information from an innovator.

❦ DIFFUSION OF AN INNOVATION ❦

Having identified some of the components which might influence the rate of diffusion of an innovation, we can assemble

30

them and emerge with a possible theoretical framework for our analysis. Again, Rogers provides a good source for this purpose. To begin with, he divides the components of the theoretical system into three parts: antecedents, process, and results.

Two major types of antecedents are identifiable: (1) the individual's identity, including his sense of security, his dominant values, his mental ability and conceptual skill, his social status, and his cosmopolite orientation; and (2) the individual's perception of the social system surrounding him, including its norms for innovation, economic constraints and incentives, and its nature and function.

The process itself is divided into five stages: awareness, interest, evaluation, trial, and adoption (or rejection). The nature of information sources and the perceived characteristics of an innovation are important to the outcome of the process. Seemingly, cosmopolitan sources—for example, mass media—are most important in the early stages when the individual becomes aware of an innovation mainly through impersonal sources. Perceived characteristics emerge at the mid-point of the process, the evaluation stage; at this point, local- and personal-information sources become more important.

The diffusion process results in either adoption or rejection of an idea. If adopted, an innovation may be used continuously, or rejected at a later date. Although Rogers does not specifically point to what we have called the "reversion phenomenon," the "experimental" adoption—which, in fact, cannot be considered a complete adoption at all—could be viewed as belonging to the category in which an idea is first adopted, then later rejected. The possibility exists, as Rogers points out, that the innovation is rejected at the end of the process, but adopted at a later date. Of course, the innovation can be continuously rejected.

We hope that even our limited discussion of previous observations concerning the diffusion of innovation shows, when applied to higher education, how easily a number of significant hy-

31

potheses can be generated. From such hypotheses emerges the kind of theoretical model which might help set the stage for our own investigation and assist us in interpreting some of our findings. We also hope that we have developed a further perspective from which to view the following chapters.

THREE

RESEARCH SETTING FOR INNOVATION

Slightly more than five decades ago, the Russian Boris Rosing and the Englishman A. A. Campbell-Swinton independently suggested that cathode rays could be used to reconstruct an image transmitted electronically. This discovery was to become the cornerstone of one of the most fantastic technical developments of our century.

These cathode tubes, major components in our television sets, project the kaleidoscopic events of our world to us.

During one year alone, this amazing electronic device was able to provide American viewers with a front-row seat at the coronation of Pope Paul VI directly from the Vatican; show them the massive racial demonstrations in Southern and Northern metropolitan areas; and even make them eye-witnesses to the murder of a presidential assassin. The cathode tube continues to reflect man's greatest triumphs, as well as his most disastrous failures. Yet, like any technical innovation, probably beginning with the invention of the wheel, television has been viewed with suspicion and contempt—even by some segments of Western culture. It has been accused of a myriad of evils, ranging from destroying the imagination of our children to jeopardizing our judicial system. Some have referred to it as the "boob tube," the "window on a wasteland," and even made it responsible for the creation of a generation of "vidiots." Actually, it is guilty of none of these offenses. Like all technical inno-

33

vations, it depends on human beings to use it to their advantage or disadvantage. Its potential for either good or evil staggers the imagination.

❦ CHALLENGE OF INSTRUCTIONAL TELEVISION ❦

Our research case history focuses on one possible use for this modern system of communication: television as a teaching device at the college level. As we pointed out earlier, diffusion of technical innovations in the field of education has been slow and is almost always accompanied by suspicion and hostility. We find instructional television (ITV) to be no exception.[1] Although a considerable number and variety of universities are offering telecourses, both open and closed circuit, virtually all teaching institutions which have attempted to use television have encountered some difficulties. Undeniably, the possibility exists that ITV may become institutionalized in some of these schools, but the findings of our research case history and the reports from the nine universities at which we explored this medium do not augur well for those who favor ITV as a permanent teaching method in higher education.

Such resistance seems to fall into two categories: (1) an apathy or, perhaps, a feeling of irrelevancy concerning television as a teaching device and (2) an outright hostility and repudiation of ITV regardless of the manner in which it is applied. The introduction to the *Yearbook of Education* (Bereday and Lauwerys, 1960) presents this point more concisely, if less gently: "Inventions making possible the wider diffusion of knowledge have usually been attacked by power elites—the suspicion, criticism, and denigration of radio, television and cinema by the upper classes and the most highly educated classes of today may perhaps be cited as an example" (p. 8).

[1] Extensive observations relevant to this point appear both in Chapter 8, which reports on some of the reactions the authors received during their visits to nine other universities, and in the tables in Appendix 3, which reports studies of ITV at four other universities.

To the behavioral or social scientist, such suspicion and hostility toward innovations on the part of individuals or whole societies are not a new phenomenon. While some social scientists examine the social structure to find explanations for it, the social psychologist tends to examine more closely the behavior of the individual within that structure. Thus, he has been able to demonstrate that the individual's perception of one specific artifact in his environment is conditioned to a large extent by the feelings he has toward other artifacts. In all likelihood, such feelings may be rooted in a highly complex network of fears, suspicions, and ignorance, as students of the irrational nature of attitudes point out (for example, Krech and Crutchfield, 1948).

As we will show, many of the negative attitudes which educators display toward ITV are not always based on rational evaluations with a maximum of knowledge but, rather, are emotional responses to a contrived image vaguely perceived as a threat. Nor can such accusations of irrationality be hurled only against those who are hostile to instructional television. The euphoria of those who see ITV as a panacea that will solve all the problems of higher education is often based on equally irrational reasoning. An investigation by Rokeach, Smith, and Evans (1960) suggests the possibility that dogmatic beliefs like the ones reflected in the present study on ITV (either pro- or anti-ITV) may be as important in the individual's frame of reference in a given situation as attitudes with which society is more typically concerned, such as racial or religious prejudice.

We were somewhat dismayed that a few who read the preliminary report of this study (Evans, Smith, and Colville, 1963) considered it an attempt to build a case for the use of television instruction. We hope, at the outset, that the present report will not be viewed in this sense. However, we are operating on the premise that the extent to which television can provide some of the answers to problems now facing American higher education is partly governed by the attitudes of administrators, students, and—

35

perhaps most significantly—professors toward employing it in university teaching.

Although a number of explorations into the values, attitudes, and beliefs of the university professor have appeared in recent years, these seem to be, for the most part, rather limited in scope and too often not based on research, despite the fact that they are often quite interesting. Extensive empirical investigations of values, beliefs, and attitudes involving members of university faculties as subjects have apparently been only rarely undertaken.[2] Furthermore, although some investigations have been made of faculty attitudes toward instructional television (ITV) in particular,[3] these have frequently been limited to a relatively simple descriptive level of analysis. In fact, Kumata (1960) refers to such research when he states that "There is a tendency for research to be an afterthought to instructional television efforts. Except in a very few studies, a true partnership between performance and evaluation does not exist" (p. 235).

❧ AIMS AND ISSUES ❧

Aside from viewing faculty reactions to instructional television as an interesting case history in the social psychology of innovation, we designed our study to accomplish three major goals:

1. To examine certain interesting attitudes and values of an urban university faculty in general and to provide a specific analytic focus on ITV attitudes.
2. To evaluate techniques of overcoming ITV resistance in a departmental group as a means of testing hypotheses that are implicit in certain social psychological theories of attitude change.
3. To examine, by the use of a battery of tests, interviews, and

---

[2] For example, the writers have recently become aware that such a study is currently being undertaken by the Association for Higher Education of the National Education Association.

[3] A representative sample of these appears in Appendix 3.

analyses, the relationships between general faculty attitudes and extreme attitudes toward ITV.

In the pursuit of these three basic goals, our aim was to seek answers to the following questions:

1. What is the nature and extent of attitudes held by a university faculty toward the prospect of teaching by television?
2. In what way are these ITV attitudes interrelated with other attitudes and values inherent in the university's social and intellectual climate?
3. In what ways are professors who are strongly favorable to teaching by ITV different from those who are strongly hostile to it?
4. As a theoretical exploration of the dynamics of attitude change, to what degree can Festinger's and Carlsmith's "forced-compliance" model (1959) applied to a faculty group involved in the use of ITV modify the professors' attitudes toward this innovation?
5. What promise does the video-tape recorder, as used in the faculty-participation situation described above, hold as a device for improving teaching?

Aside, then, from providing an example of the process of diffusion of an innovation in higher education, our research case history deals on a social psychological level with a hopefully more extensive and empirical exploration of a faculty's values, attitudes, and beliefs than previous reports reflect. The present investigation is further directed toward exploring the conditions which may modify attitudes toward a specific innovation, such as teaching by television.

The investigators had no illusions about the difficulties inherent in their task. Unlike the chemist, who can always observe with detachment the behavior of certain chemicals in a test tube, the social psychologist in an investigation like ours may find himself personally confronted with the subjects whose behavior he is observing. The case is greatly accentuated in an exploration of controversial issues. Thus, we were aware that the hostility toward

ITV by faculty members who frequently saw it as a threat to job security would also be directed toward any attempt to "intrude" into their privately held opinions or to manipulate their attitudes. McKeachie (1962) points to this problem when he says, "Since some college faculty members are anxious about technological unemployment and resist innovations, research has often been used as a technique of infiltration, rather than as a method of developing and testing theory" (p. 342). Some of our subjects may very well, then, have considered our research case history as being simultaneously directed toward both the testing of theory and infiltrating. Obviously, we did not have the latter goal in mind. To minimize this problem, we made efforts to brief our subjects concerning the ethics of the psychologist in this type of research, which would preclude, among other things, such infiltration. They were also assured of the complete anonymity of their responses.

❦ METHODS AND TECHNIQUES ❦

Chronologically, our investigation began with the development of an initial questionnaire, which we sent to the entire full-time faculty of Metro University. This device consisted of three major parts. The first section requested information on the professional and academic background of the respondent, as well as other biographical material.

The second section of our questionnaire utilized an especially adapted form of the Osgood Semantic Differential designed by Osgood, Suci, and Tannenbaum (1957).[4] This technique, which is widely used in psychological measurement, requires that the respondent rate a particular concept as being more closely related to one or the other of a set of bipolar adjective pairs, such as *bad-good* and *rough-smooth*. Each concept for which an attitude measurement is attempted is rated on a sequence of such adjective pairs, which have been selected by a systematic analysis as

---

[4] We wish to thank Charles Osgood for the valuable suggestions he made concerning the use of the Semantic Differential prior to the beginning of the project.

the most fundamentally meaningful for the individual. Each pair is divided along a seven-point scale; three points indicate the degree of *each* of the opposing adjectives, while a theoretical neutral point indicates that neither adjective has a connotation related to a particular concept.

We selected 30 concepts to be used with such adjective pairs, which were designed to explore attitudes toward a representative group of items implicit or critical within the total university situation. Five of these were directly related to instructional television (ITV); the rest might or might not bear an indirect relationship to these attitudes. Included among these latter concepts were night students, athletic scholarships, emphasis on research, and state support for the University.[5] One sample item and its scale are reproduced below:

Metro University becoming a state university

good ——— : ——— : ——— : ——— : ——— : ——— : ——— bad

By using this standardized, quantifiable method, we could assign measurable valences for each subject from his response to each concept. The Semantic Differential also has clusters of adjective pairs designed to provide measures for different components of meaning. Previous factor analyses of data obtained by this technique have revealed at least three such components for which such separate scales are relevant. It provides an evaluative scale, expressed by such adjective pairs as *good-bad;* a potency scale, expressed by such adjective pairs as *weak-strong;* and, finally, an activity scale, which might be expressed by the adjective pair *slow-fast.*

We selected the scales for the present study from a compilation of such adjective pairs (Jenkins and Russell, 1958) for which factor loading was determined, that is, the extent to which each pair may contribute to the variability of the response. The criterion for the choice of the particular pairs was, of course, their relevance to both the specific ITV-related concepts and the more general

[5] For a complete list of items, see Appendix 1.

items of local importance to the university community, as well as the relative size of their factor loadings. The scales selected were

Evaluative Scale

Good _____ Bad

Dishonest _____ Honest

Unfair _____ Fair

Unpleasant _____ Pleasant

Worthless _____ Valuable

Potency Scale

Rough _____ Smooth

Weak _____ Strong

Soft _____ Hard

Activity Scale

Passive _____ Active

Slow _____ Fast

In another part of the study, all the Semantic Differential responses were subjected to a factor analysis. This statistical method, which is used for large groups of responses to diverse concepts, tries to ferret out those which are interrelated or overlapping, and thus identifies the generic attitudes which underlie such clusters. It is possible in this manner to reduce a large number of variables to a relatively small number of factors which account for the common variance in the original data. For example, factor analysis has been used to determine the extent to which verbal facility is a factor common to a variety of intelligence tests. Although this analysis was completed to provide additional insight into the nature of response constellations, it also allowed us to validate further the evaluative, activity, and potency factors of the Semantic Differential within the context of our research case history. This portion of the study is reported in Chapter 5, and additional details of the factor analysis are reported in Appendix 2.

In the third and final section of the faculty questionnaire, respondents were asked to indicate which of 14 teaching methods they preferred to use in introductory courses with large enrollments and which techniques from a varied list they used to evaluate student performance. Two of these were related to ITV.

Our staff carefully selected each item in the initial questionnaire with the hope of discovering all possible facets of the total university teaching situation—facets which would reflect the various values and attitudes professors had regarding this situation, as well as the range of teaching techniques which they used. Prior to administering the questionnaire to the total faculty, we asked a sample of young psychology instructors for a critical evaluation of it. From their suggestions, a second form was developed and likewise evaluated.

Although from the outset the study was not designed to study students' attitudes extensively, 45 class members in an introductory psychology course were asked to respond to a slightly modified version of the last two sections of the questionnaire, so that a comparison of faculty and student answers could be made on some items, even if in an exploratory manner.

Since we realized that even this administration of our initial questionnaire was unique within a university, we knew that it might not yield a very high return from faculty members without a special effort on our part. With such effort we were fortunate enough to obtain a return from 80 per cent of the total faculty, 319 responses out of a possible 400. This special effort involved obtaining permission from the Dean of Faculties to administer the questionnaire (as is normally the case with such materials, the Dean's approval was indicated on the face of the form) and, through personal contact, repeatedly encouraging faculty members slow to respond to return the completed questionnaire. Since the "no-return" group was so small, the data obtained were probably representative of the entire faculty. (Even though we made no study in depth to determine the possibility that the "no-return" members were atypical, simple demographic comparisons of this group with the "return" group did not suggest this probability.)

The next step in the procedure was to select two groups falling at opposite extremes on the basis of their responses to the spe-

41

cific ITV questions. Analysis of the questionnaires showed that the concept of *Television in large-enrollment classes* evoked the most unqualified reaction on the *good-bad, weak-strong,* and *valuable-worthless* scales. Therefore, the responses to this question became the basis for establishing two extreme groups:

Pro-ITV's   (55 faculty members most favorable to instructional television)

Anti-ITV's   (65 faculty members most hostile to instructional television)

Imbedded within the two groups above was a third one we will designate as our experimental group (EXP-ITV). Its 20 members represented two departments in the College of Arts and Sciences. These departments were selected for the experimental portion of the study because they had previously rejected official overtures from the Administration to use ITV in their required introductory courses with large enrollments. As a result of extended explorations which the senior author had made prior to the investigation, these two departments agreed to participate in the experimental-operational phase of the study. These 20 professors (comprised of 9 members of one department and 11 of the other) made up the group which would ultimately be involved in the experimental phase of the research case history. A more detailed description of this phase of the study will be presented in Chapter 7. For the present the reader must only keep in mind that this was one of the experimental groups which would provide the data for testing some of our hypotheses regarding attitude change.

To supplement our self-administered initial questionnaire, we developed two schedules for personal interviews prior to and after the experimental phase. Using some of the typical guidelines that Maccoby and Maccoby (1954) describe, we carefully designed these interview schedules to elicit, through standardized open-end, fixed-alternative, and projective questions, more intensive responses from the anti- and pro-ITV groups about their values, attitudes, beliefs, and other personality characteristics. Because of its particular relevance, in the case of the items in the interviews dealing with teaching machines and instructional television, we used a special adaptation of a "cognitive role-playing" device prepared by Evans (1952). This is an indirect measure of attitudes, which hopefully eliminates some defensiveness in respondents.

Before conducting these interviews with our subjects, we pretested the interview forms on a group of six young instructors in psychology, with the idea of getting their critical evaluations. From these evaluations, we revised and constructed the interviews in a final form. Because of the unusual nature of our sample, a team of three clinical psychology professors were recruited to complete the personal interviews with each of the professors in the anti- and pro-ITV groups.

Analysis of data obtained in the interviews was handled through the typical content-analysis procedures that Berelson (1954) describes. Three members of the research staff, who were psychology graduate students, served as the original coding group as a first step in the content analysis of the responses. These coders independently set up response categories for the open-end interview responses. They then met together and, on the basis of independent external criteria, determined to what degree their response categories were consistent with one another. To a surprising degree we found that they had arrived at very similar response categories. Therefore, after being subjected to a few more trial-and-error modifications, certain categories seemed to emerge as being adequate.

Using these established-response categories, the three raters again coded the responses from the pretest and posttest interviews. Occasionally, when certain responses could not be easily coded, an arbitrary decision was made to consider an agreement pattern of two out of three as adequate. Interestingly enough, this kind of arbitrary decision was unnecessary most of the time; the response categories set up by our research-staff coding group seemed to be quite sufficient. The overall agreement in coding among the three raters of the pretest interview was 76.6 per cent, and for the posttest interview, 78.5 per cent.

43

❧ METRO UNIVERSITY ❧

A brief description of the history and present status of the Metro University community may orient our total study; at the same time, it may set some limits to the degree that our findings can be generalized. Metro is a fairly young institution located in a rapidly growing urban area. Its rapid growth and development are somewhat typical for institutions of higher education in such environments.

At the time of this study, Metro University was receiving some state support, and increasing sentiment, both among its own staff and within the community at large, was in favor of seeking full state support—a change which has since been obtained. The general feeling was that such a transition would bring a reduction in the tuition charges and, hence, an increased enrollment. This anticipation was confirmed by later developments; enrollment increased by 50 per cent during the first year of state support.

We should point out, for purposes of this study, that Metro University operated one of the first educational-television stations. During the first year of this operation, nine telecourses were presented. During subsequent years, telecourses included three freshman courses—biology, mathematics, and psychology—and three sophomore courses—English, accounting, and political science. All of these were credit courses requiring that the students watch two television lectures and attend one class session per week. Some 4,000 to 6,000 students a year were instructed by this method. Later, all university telecourses were terminated for lack of adequate state support of the television system. Eventual termination, however, is a typical pattern in most universities which begin television courses, but the reasons for it ostensibly differ.

When we were making our investigation, approximately 13,000 students attended Metro and were instructed by a faculty of around 400 full-time members. As is fairly typical for institutions of this type, most of the students, who were older than those

44

normally found on a resident college campus, lived at home or, at least, resided off campus. Many held part-time jobs in the community. But since our investigation is focused primarily on the faculty, a more detailed analysis of its members is in order now.

Responses to the initial questionnaire provided considerable insight into the general characteristics and professional status of the Metro faculty. Again, the composite picture does not seem unusual for a relatively young, urban university. Eight out of ten of those who responded to the questionnaire were males, who on the average were 40 years old and had 2.75 dependents. They carried a teaching load averaging 10.25 semester hours, with 12 hours given as the most frequent. Interestingly enough, although 15 respondents failed to answer the question concerning age, 30 did not respond to the question about their teaching load. Half the faculty had less than 10 years' teaching experience, with the average slightly above 13 years. There were only 11 per cent who had not earned a degree higher than the baccalaureate, while 42 per cent had earned a master's degree and 47 per cent had earned their doctorate.

Another index for measuring academic and professional status—one which has increased in importance in recent years—is the degree to which faculty members contribute to professional journals and participate in professional organizations. Of those who responded to questions concerning these activities, about half reported that they had published from 1 to 78 papers, with an average of slightly over 6; and, again, over half had presented papers at professional meetings, the number of these ranging from 1 to 30, with an average of 5.

Perhaps this brief sketch of Metro University and its faculty at the time of our study will convey something of the background against which our research case history should be viewed. Although no two institutions are precisely alike, we believe that Metro is fairly similar in many respects to other urban centers of higher education.

FOUR

PROFILE
OF A
UNIVERSITY
FACULTY

Contemporary social psychological theory (for example, Krech, Crutchfield, and Ballachey, 1962) suggests that few, if any, of an individual's attitudes exist in complete isolation, although they do vary extensively in the degree and kind of patterns in which they are intercorrelated. Often we find such relationships in the person's values, beliefs, opinions, and attitudes directed toward a variety of both similar and disparate social objects. For example, in an early work on authoritarianism (Adorno, Frenkel-Brunswik, Levinson, and Sanford, 1950), attitudes toward various minority groups are related to various political attitudes. However, to say that such a constellation of values, beliefs, opinions, and attitudes always forms a unified whole would be a great oversimplification, although the degree to which unity exists may indicate the degree of consistency in the individual's ideology. At the same time, considerable evidence shows conflicting attitudes, even toward the same item. Some writers (for example, Krech and Crutchfield, 1948) refer to some of these inconsistent attitudes as "logic-tight compartments." A person, for instance, may assert the belief that all individuals should have equal rights but, in a slightly different context, appear to believe with equal firmness that the rights of some should be abridged.

In recent years numerous investigations have attempted to

show that one of the basic personality traits affecting a person's perception of social objects is the extent to which he relies upon authoritarian or equalitarian beliefs. The work we mentioned above on authoritarianism (Adorno *et al.*) identifies the following as personality traits that either contribute to high authoritarianism or are interrelated with it: rigid adherence to and exaggerated concern for conventional middle-class values; condemnation and rejection of those who violate conventional values; preoccupation with figures of authority and power; and hostility toward members of outgroups.

❦ *FACULTY PERSONALITY* ❦

We felt that an examination of the authoritarian-equalitarian traits of our respondents might suggest some characteristics related to faculty attitudes toward such innovations as instructional television. Thus, we included two projective questions from Adorno's and his colleagues' work on authoritarianism in the pretest-interview schedule, items which appeared to be at least peripheral measures of authoritarianism. We believed these items could easily be adapted to our interview and would not be too offensive to our respondents. They were

What great people both living or dead do you admire the most?

What experiences give you the greatest feeling of awe?

We then analyzed the content of the responses, using as a base the categories that Adorno and his colleagues suggest.

In response to the first question, according to the above classification, 59 respondents ranked high in authoritarianism, while 35 ranked medium and 24 low. In response to the second question, 47 ranked high, 47 ranked medium, while, again, 24 ranked low. However, these data should be interpreted on the basis that we used only two items dealing with authoritarianism from a far more elaborate group designed to measure this variable. Evidently, no significant differences in authoritarianism existed be-

47

tween the extreme groups. However, since we had no data for authoritarianism on our middle group (neither pro- nor anti-ITV), it is difficult to assess this finding, except that it suggests at least as high an incidence of authoritarianism in our faculty sample as occurs in less select populations.

The present interview also included an item that asked faculty members to evaluate the original questionnaire in general and also for their reaction to being interviewed. This evaluation was designed to generate an attitude which might be called "re-action to intrusiveness," or what Adorno and his colleagues describe as "anti-intraceptiveness." Anti-intraceptiveness implies little tendency to introspect or to gain insight into the psychological and social mechanisms of one's self and others. Adorno and his colleagues point out that the anti-intraceptive individual is afraid of what might be revealed if he or others should look too closely at himself. He opposes people's "prying" into his affairs, but, yet, he is insensitive to what others think and feel. Instead of making unnecessary "talk," he prefers to keep busy and devote himself to practical pursuits. He implies that he would prefer to think about something cheerful rather than examine inner conflicts. But we need to emphasize that these are not the only reasons why a person may react unfavorably to such intrusions.[1] However, one interpretation of the responses of our faculty interviewees to the original questionnaire could be an indication of anti-intraceptiveness.

Since this reaction is also related to authoritarianism (Adorno *et al.*), the responses here tended to confirm the findings from the projective questions measuring authoritarianism. Only 75 favorable responses were given; among these the most frequent (21) was that they liked the questionnaire because it was easy to answer, clear, and easily understood. Against this, 198 unfavorable

---

[1] Proshansky and Evans (1963), dealing with political extremist groups, recognize that reaction to intrusiveness should not be interpreted as being necessarily "bad." Obviously, rational reasons can exist for resenting intrusions of one's privacy.

responses were counted, with 84 professors disliking the questionnaire because it was ambiguous, confusing, and unclear. In part, this reaction was due to the indirect nature of the Semantic Differential as described by Osgood, Suci, and Tannenbaum (1957). In fact, we were surprised that so few respondents reacted to the ambiguity of the form.

In both the pretest and posttest interviews, our interviewees provided further data about the individual behavior of faculty members based on summaries of their ratings. For this purpose, three nine-point a priori scales which we had designated recorded interviewers' estimates of each subject's personality in terms of being secure or evasive, tolerant or hostile, and sophisticated or bland. A value of 1 was assigned to the first concept in each dimension, and 9 for the second. Independent ratings of these summaries by three other people showed high-agreement coefficients of .77 among all the raters.

The mean of these ratings for each dimension ranged from 5.28 to 5.47. Since 5, of course, was a neutral point, this indicated that the respondents were only slightly evasive, hostile, or bland during the interviews. Under the circumstances as we have presented them, these data, which reflect a fairly high degree of cooperation from faculty members, are a tribute to the skill of our interviewing staff.

It is undoubtedly clear by now that the present study proceeded from the assumption that the attitudes which most of our faculty members held toward ITV did not exist in isolation but were often interconnected in varying degrees with other attitudes, such as those toward teaching machines and teaching methods versus content. They were even interconnected with the respondent's attitude toward himself and his general philosophy of life. A clearer picture of these relationships will emerge from the data on factor analysis reported in the next chapter. These data will also point to some apparent inconsistencies in our respondents' attitudes.

❦ *PROFESSOR'S SELF-IMAGE* ❦

Table 1 shows the overall means of the evaluative scales of the Semantic Differential from the original questionnaire.[2] The

TABLE 1

OVERALL MEANS OF OSGOOD EVALUATIVE SCALES
RANKED FROM MOST TO LEAST FAVORABLE

Rank	Item	Overall Mean (Evaluative Scales)
1.	Myself conducting a small class	5.99
2.	Myself as a professor	5.80
3.	Myself conducting an advanced course	5.76
4.	Myself conducting an introductory course	5.67
5.	Myself conducting a lecture course	5.61
6.	Night students	5.49
7.	Higher entrance requirements for university	5.48
8.	University becoming a state university	5.48
9.	Larger salary increases with fewer additional fringe benefits	5.46
10.	Emphasis on research at university	5.39
11.	Lecture method supplemented by small discussion sections for large classes	5.38
12.	Myself conducting a large class	5.34
13.	Myself doing publishable research	5.23
14.	Training in teaching methods for prospective professors	5.02
15.	Admitting qualified Negroes to the university	4.95
16.	Answering students' questions in large classes	4.94
17.	Training in teaching methods for professors	4.87
18.	Television instruction supplemented by small discussion	4.73
19.	Metro Festival (student activity)	4.56
20.	Myself conducting a television course	4.42

[2] A more detailed presentation of these data appears in Evans, Smith, and Colville (1962).

Rank	Item	Overall Mean (Evaluative Scales)
21.	Honor courses consisting only of textbooks and final examinations	4.21
22.	Teaching machines	4.07
23.	Television instruction in introductory courses	4.02
	THEORETICALLY NEUTRAL ON OSGOOD SCALES	4.00
24.	Athletic scholarships	3.99
25.	Straight lecture method for large classes	3.96
26.	Correspondence courses	3.84
27.	More fringe benefits with smaller salary increase	3.83
28.	Additional tuition	3.73
29.	Television instruction in advanced courses	3.57
30.	Straight television instruction for large classes	3.48

items are ranked from the most favorable to the least favorable. Even a cursory examination of the items relating to the professors' self-concepts shows that the Metro faculty was, on the whole, self-confident about its instructional skills. On the combined basis of the first three items, our respondents clearly saw themselves in a favorable light as college professors teaching a small, advanced course; they ranked, however, the conducting of a large class or doing publishable research considerably lower. We can note further that they ranked all items dealing directly with ITV in the lower half of the list, reserving their lowest ranking for television instruction in advanced courses or "straight" in large classes. However, when the professor was asked to project himself into a teaching situation using television, his opinion of the medium rose significantly. Apparently, the "myself" component of that concept weighted the item in a more favorable direction.

Because faculty members thought so highly of themselves as professors, we decided—as mentioned in the last chapter—to administer a similar questionnaire to a sampling of 45 students in an introductory psychology course to see whether they evaluated the faculty in the same favorable light. We asked them to respond to 14 items from our original questionnaire, with the "myself" items changed to read, "Most professors I have had at the university." An overall evaluation of these responses, shown in Table 2, indicates that the students' evaluation is fairly consistent with that of the faculty, at least as far as ranking goes. However, a more subtle analysis of the results indicates clearly that students rated the faculty lower than the faculty rated itself. This may be seen in Figure 1, which is based on projections from the data.

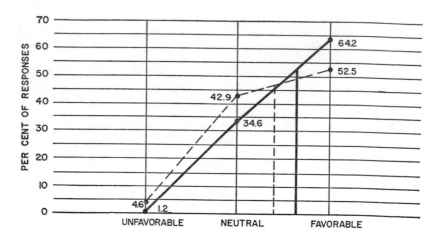

FIGURE 1. Comparison of faculty and student Semantic Differential responses to the concept "Myself (most professors) conducting an introductory course." (Solid line represents faculty responses; broken line represents student responses.)

❧ COURSE CONTENT AND TEACHING METHODS ❧

With this picture of the personality makeup and self-image of the Metro faculty, we are ready to consider those attitudes which are more specifically related to teaching. As every college student or alumnus knows, the methods and techniques which professors

TABLE 2(A)

OVERALL MEAN EVALUATIVE-SCALE RESPONSES OF PROFESSORS AND STUDENTS AND CHI SQUARE TESTS BASED ON RESPONSE FREQUENCIES

Item	Professors	Students	Chi Square	p
Myself as a professor (Most professors I have had at Metro University)	5.80	5.60	39.86	.001
Myself conducting an introductory course (Most professors at Metro University conducting an introductory course)	5.67	5.51	26.18	.001
Myself conducting a lecture course (Most professors I have had at Metro University conducting a lecture course)	5.61	5.20	56.66	.001
Lecture method supplemented by small discussion sections for large classes	5.38	5.64	12.30	.01
Myself conducting a television course (Most professors conducting a television course)	4.42	4.92	87.82	.001
Television instruction in introductory courses	4.02	3.72	54.24	.001
Straight television instruction for large classes	3.48	3.41	43.96	.001

Significant differences were found on all seven items tested, although the relative ranking of items was approximately the same within both groups.

TABLE 2(B)

MEAN EVALUATIVE-SCALE VALUES AND RANKINGS OF STUDENT
RESPONSES TO 14 ITEMS AS COMPARED WITH PROFESSORS' RESPONSES

Item	Students' Means	Rank	Professors' Means (Item in "Myself" Terms)	Rank
Most professors at Metro University conducting a small class	6.03	1	5.99	1
Lecture method supplemented by small discussion sections for large classes	5.64	2	5.38	6
Most professors I have had at Metro University	5.60	3	5.80	2
Most professors at Metro University conducting an introductory course	5.51	4	5.67	4
Most professors at Metro University conducting an advanced course	5.44	5	5.76	3
Most professors at Metro University conducting a large class	5.33	6	5.34	7
Most professors I have had at Metro University conducting a lecture course	5.20	7	5.61	5
Television instruction supplemented by small discussion sections for large classes	5.19	8	4.73	8
Most professors conducting a television course	4.92	9	4.42	9
Teaching machines	4.30	10	4.07	10
Straight lecture method for large classes	3.97	11	3.96	12
Television instruction in introductory courses	3.72	12	4.02	11
Television instruction in advanced courses	3.53	13	3.57	13
Straight television instruction for large classes	3.41	14	3.48	14

54

use to present material and evaluate student performance vary greatly. Our data tend to support this; furthermore, most of our respondents felt that the methods they were using were particularly suited to the courses which they were teaching, and although they were aware that others were using different methods, they felt that these would not work for their subjects or their students. We also find that university professors—again, not unlike other members of professional groups—tend to be conservative, favoring old, tried-and-true methods and viewing innovations of any kind with considerable apprehension.

Should a professor, in addition to being competently acquainted with the material he is teaching, also have training in teaching methods? This question always generates rather heated discussion. The fact is that virtually no university requires prospective professors to obtain training in teaching methods. Presumably, the student at this level, in contrast to the primary and secondary pupil, is capable of comprehending material regardless of how it is presented. In response to a pretest-interview question on the comparative value of content and method of teaching, most of our respondents apparently agreed with the prevailing opinions. Forty per cent believed that knowledge of content is a sufficient prerequisite for university teaching, although 35 per cent felt that method is of some importance and 10 per cent felt that they are of equal importance. Ten per cent gave ambiguous responses. These figures are quite a contrast to the 5 per cent who felt method to be more important than content. On a subjective level, we might legitimately infer from these data that our respondents not only considered content more important than method in university teaching but that, even though they might lack training in methods, they had sufficient knowledge of content to make them good professors. Continuing in this risky vein, we might cautiously add that our respondents seemed to feel that ITV would require knowledge of teaching methods or might possibly expose inadequate methods to a viewing audience—an audience which might include fellow faculty members and administrators.

55

Does the above mean that teaching methods were unimportant to our respondents at Metro? To say so would be a mistake. As a matter of fact, our respondents placed training in teaching methods for prospective and present professors fairly high on the evaluative scale, with means 5.02 and 4.89 respectively. These figures indicate some considerable concern about method in spite of the heavy emphasis on content.

Our original questionnaire probed more deeply to find specifically what the preferred teaching methods were, and, again, we compared the instructors' ratings with those of a group of 45 students in an introductory psychology class. Table 3 shows these preferences ranked from the most to the least preferred. These results clearly indicate a preference by professors for those methods

TABLE 3

COMPARISON OF TEACHING METHODS PREFERRED BY PROFESSORS AND STUDENTS

(Preference in order from most to least. Ranking of 1, most used and favored; 2, next preference, etc.)

Teaching Method	Instructor Rating (n = 319)	Student Rating (n = 45)
Classroom lectures	1	2.5
Use of blackboard	2	2.5
Outside work or readings in addition to textbook	3	9.5
Class demonstrations	4	1
Motion pictures	5	4
Supplementary small discussion	6	5
Guest instructors	7	6
Slides	8	12
Supplementary viewing (occasionally) of ITV	9	8
Field trips	10	7
Private tutorial sessions	11	9.5
Socratic method	12	14
Television lectures	13	11
Teaching machines	14	13

which cast the university teacher in his traditional role: standing before the class, giving a lecture, using the blackboard, assigning some outside homework, and occasionally giving a classroom demonstration. The only surprising factor is the relatively high rank, fifth place, that the professor gave motion pictures. Perhaps this rating indicates an innovation which has achieved some degree of acceptance as a communication medium. On the other hand, they again rated television lectures and teaching machines lowest.

Apparently, the students pretty much agreed with their professors about these methods. Their ratings, with the exception of those for outside work or readings in addition to textbooks, indicate that they felt satisfied with the methods used for presenting material to them. However, they rated class demonstration above all other methods and ranked television lectures slightly higher than their teachers did.[3]

❧ *TEACHING MACHINES* ❧

One teaching method which deserves a more detailed analysis is teaching machines. We believed that these devices would be related to ITV as a focal point of faculty resistance. As we mentioned earlier, in the original questionnaire our respondents ranked teaching machines lowest among the teaching methods they preferred, even lower than television lectures. When the concept appeared among the 30 Semantic Differential items, it was again ranked barely above the theoretically neutral point, with an evaluative mean of 4.07. The graphic presentation in Figure 2 shows how closely this item was rated in all dimensions to the neutral point.

The lack of variability within these results seems to indicate the probability that our Semantic Differential Scale was inadequate

---

[3] Because we selected these students from one particular section of a specific course, introductory psychology, they do *not* in any sense constitute a representative sample of students in general or even students enrolled at Metro University.

EVALUATIVE	1	2	3	4	5	6	7	
BAD						●		GOOD
DISHONEST						●		HONEST
UNFAIR						●		FAIR
UNPLEASANT					●			PLEASANT
WORTHLESS					●			VALUABLE
POTENCY								
ROUGH				●				SMOOTH
WEAK					●			STRONG
SOFT				●				HARD
ACTIVITY								
PASSIVE					●			ACTIVE
SLOW					●			FAST

FIGURE 2. Graphic representation of mean-scale values for the Semantic Differential concept "Myself as a professor."

for measuring this item. On the other hand, the provocative responses resulting from the inclusion of questions on teaching machines in the pretest interview suggest a considerable variability in the respondents' feelings toward them. Of the 120 interviewees in the pro-ITV and anti-ITV groups, 67 were opposed to such devices, while 29 favored them, and 24 held no opinion. To get at the reasons for this faculty resistance, the interviewers probed more deeply.

Instead of simply asking the respondent how he personally felt about teaching machines and why, we adapted the special role-playing technique developed by Evans (1952). This technique consists of what we might call "cognitive role playing." After the respondent is asked to imagine himself opposed to some social object, he is then asked to imagine himself in favor of it. This technique, we decided, might be interesting in examining attitudes toward the teaching machine and instructional television, since it permitted an additional opportunity for more qualitative responses.

To begin with, the interviewees were asked if they were acquainted with teaching machines; if not, they were given a short, simple description. These devices, it was explained, are auto-instructional and present to the student a series of problems reflecting a given subject-matter area. Each student proceeds at his own rate and must solve each problem in a programmed sequence. Because of the way the machines are constructed, he is provided with immediate knowledge of his progress. The student cannot advance without completing each step of the program. After this explanation, the respondent was asked to imagine himself first opposed to teaching machines and then in favor of them, stating in each case as many different reasons as possible for his position.

While imagining themselves in favor of teaching machines, the interviewees offered 269 responses. About half of them felt that these devices might be good for drill and practice and might even overcome the teacher shortage by reaching more students. About one fifth felt that the machines provide dependability and a method for more standardized teaching. On the other hand, when the respondents imagined themselves as being opposed to these devices, they were able to think of 290 reasons for their opposition. Most of them, nearly three fourths, felt that the machines are too impersonal and provide no opportunity for discussion, while about one fourth felt that since machines lack creativity and can only handle facts, they cannot motivate students. Clearly, these reasons for opposing the machines support the high evaluation of the "myself" items in Table 1. In effect, the professors were saying, "The machine cannot provide those ingredients which I, myself, can provide. I am personal and provide discussion; I motivate students; and I am creative." Undoubtedly, the quasi role-playing technique served as a valuable means of soliciting this great variety of responses.

❦ *UNIVERSITY-LEVEL TEACHING* ❦

During one of the two interviews, by obtaining answers to open-end questions, we attempted to validate the responses to the fixed-alternative questions. In addition to gaining some information concerning the validity of our initial questionnaire in this way, we obtained additional data. For example, one of the questions in the posttest interview was "What do you believe good university-level teaching really consists of?" We received 287 responses to this item. Sixty-three respondents stated, again as before, that "The teacher should know content and keep up with research"; for 55 respondents good preparation and use of methods were essential. Forty-three emphasized pleasant personality and interest in students, while 36 felt that a good teacher should inspire his classes. Considerable doubt exists as to whether students would agree that this hierarchy of attributes is a prerequisite for good university teaching. Evans (1962) finds that "ability to communicate" is the single most important characteristic that students seek in an instructor. Factors such as research by the professor are considered far less important.

Continuing to use the technique of quasi role playing, the interviewers then moved to another question. "Imagine for the moment that you are the dean of a college," they asked, "and you wish to improve the teaching faculty. What approach would you take with this problem?" "Give reward of money and recognition" was the method that 48 respondents proposed. Forty answered with "hire competent teachers," while 28 said they would "require refresher courses and further study." Twenty-two placed value on "in-class observation and approval of lesson plans," and 18 others proposed that they would "gather student opinions." Interdepartmental meetings and group discussion were suggested by 16. Interestingly enough, this question produced only one response category which was even slightly related to ITV. In this category 12 respondents suggested "use of audio-visual aids, including tele-

60

vision." Obviously, even the strongest proponents of ITV did not visualize its use in the context of improving teaching. Perhaps most fascinating is the fact that 16 professors stated that they would find it impossible to improve the teaching faculty.

❧ STUDENT PERFORMANCE ❧

Actually, the student is far more concerned with his professor's method of evaluating performance than with his teaching methods. At least at the undergraduate level, the questions that students ask during the first session of each semester are sure to emphasize the instructor's testing procedures. What should be the criteria by which a professor evaluates student performance? Which aspect of performance should he measure? So-called objective tests provide some indication of the student's ability to recognize material covered and discriminate among items learned, but, generally, they require little or no original thought. They are easy to correct, and grading can be on a purely objective basis. Both Metro faculty members and students rated this method highest. As a matter of fact, Table 4 shows that, again, amazing instructor-student agreement occurs. Furthermore, there is consensus on ratings of essay tests (both Metro professors and students rated them "low"). We would have assumed that instructors would have ranked such tests higher than students, because they require that the student recall, rather than recognize, material and also give some indication to what extent he has integrated this new material with his existing knowledge.

Differences of opinion did emerge on attendance, English usage, and promptness in completing assignments. While the student thought attendance ought to be among the most important criteria, the professor ranked promptness in completing assignments and three other items ahead of attendance. However, the student felt promptness in handing in assignments ranked only eighth in the group. English usage occupied a middle position in the list for

TABLE 4

COMPARISON OF EVALUATION CRITERIA PREFERRED BY
PROFESSORS AND STUDENTS

(Preference in order from most to least. Ranking of 1, most used and favored; 2, next preference, etc.)

Method of Evaluation	Instructor Rating (n = 319)	Student Rating (n = 45)
Objective tests	1	1.5
Promptness in completing assignments	2	8
Showing improvement	3	5
Essay tests	4	4
Attendance	5.5	1.5
Attitude	5.5	7
English usage	7	11.5
Themes or term papers	8	3
Spelling	9	6
Class recitation	10	9
Neatness	11	13
Tardiness	12	11.5
Extra work to raise grades	13	10
Oral examinations	14	14

the professor, but the student ranked it as one of the least important criteria for evaluating performance.

The other large discrepancy occurred in response to the item "Themes or term papers." Again, from the professor's viewpoint, these are not easy to evaluate and undoubtedly require more time than Metro faculty members felt they had available. Their rating may not indicate a judgment of this method per se; instead it may reflect upon the size of their classes, which makes this testing method impractical.

In summarizing our findings on teaching and evaluation of students, we can say that we found few, if any, surprises. The college professor sees himself in the traditional role of standing before a class, delivering a lecture on which his students take notes—notes he expects them to commit to memory, supplemented by readings in their textbooks and some additional work in the library. Periodically, he also expects them to reproduce some of this material, preferably in an easy-to-score test based on recognition and discrimination. To him it is more important that students complete assignments on time (perhaps because late papers and make-up exams require extra time) than that they be conscientious in attending lectures. The students, on the other hand, feel that they should receive some reward for faithful attendance and should not be judged too harshly when, for reasons perfectly justifiable to them, they turn in an assignment after the announced deadline.

❀ FACULTY AND UNIVERSITY ❀

Unlike most professional men—for example, physicians and lawyers—the college professor is a salaried employee of his institution. However, unlike most salaried employees, he has a highly complex relationship with his employer. We do not need to give a detailed review here of the hierarchical structure of large educational institutions, which has clearly defined roles for each member, beginning with the classroom teacher and extending to the board of trustees or even—in state-supported schools—to the state legislature. Again, unlike most employees, the university professor has an unusually high vested interest in his employer's "business." His professional status depends to a large extent on the status of the university; its fate and his are often closely intertwined. The school's academic standards add to his prestige, and the total research produced by his fellow staff members increases his stature, quite independent of his own involvement in such effort. Thus, an investigation of faculty attitudes toward university policy should prove revealing and highly relevant to the purpose of our study.

In many ways the policy problems which confront Metro University are fairly typical of most similar institutions, as we will see in a later chapter which concerns the extent to which we can

63

generalize from our data. One fairly unique problem faced Metro at the time of our study: Should it become a wholly state-supported institution? The university was aware that such a move would profoundly affect its character. Undoubtedly, the substantial decrease in tuition would result in a sharp rise in applications, which would not only increase enrollment but might provide better qualified students from the greater number of applicants. Certainly the financial position of Metro would be made more secure by state sponsorship. Some supervision by state education agencies could also be expected, which, of course, would receive a mixed response. In general, though, the feeling among Metro community members was that state sponsorship would enhance university prestige and status. In short, the overall effect of such a change would be a beneficial one. Not surprisingly, then, our respondents ranked this change fairly high on the Osgood Scale, with a mean of 5.48.

Among the questions on university policy which yielded interesting responses was the one on admitting qualified Negroes to Metro. The dimensions of *honest* and *fair,* both on the evaluative scale, received by far the highest responses. However, on the activity scales, *active-passive* and *slow-fast* received far more neutral responses, as did the potency scales of *rough-smooth, weak-strong,* and *soft-hard.* Therefore, the data would indicate that our respondents felt certain that it was *right* to admit qualified Negroes, but they were less sure about how *they* would act if and when such students were admitted. The pro-ITV professors reflected a less favorable attitude toward this item than their anti-ITV colleagues who, we would have predicted, would show a lower score because of their greater resistance to change in general. Interestingly enough, even before these data had been analyzed, Metro University quietly began admitting Negro students. Desegregation of Metro was effected without incident. This is illustrative of research possibilities in real-life settings for learning more about the observed discrepancy between cognitive and behavioral components of an attitude.

Much has been written in recent years in both popular and professional journals about the effects of the ever increasing number of prospective students knocking on the doors of already over-crowded universities. Like these institutions Metro, at the time of our investigation, was facing an immediate and substantial increase in the number of applicants for admission. Therefore, our pretest-interview question about upgrading entrance requirements as a possible solution for controlling the effects of the student-population increase was far from "academic." The majority of our respondents favored higher entrance requirements. When asked to give their reasons for this position, most felt that Metro should "pick those who are able" and "keep up a standard of quality education." Those who were against upgrading indicated most frequently that this was an "undemocratic" way to control enrollment. In passing, we may note again that not one response, even from the pro-ITV group, suggested that instructional television might alleviate the increasing classroom and teacher shortage. Hence, we will need to come back later to this question.

In the original questionnaire, the faculty as a whole favored upgrading entrance requirements even when it was not presented as a solution to the increase in applications. A positive response to this item was particularly pronounced on the evaluative scale, showing a mean of 5.48. Six respondents in the interviews expressed the opinion that upgrading should be carried on regardless of enrollment demands. An interesting note here is that a year after these data were gathered, entrance requirements were considerably upgraded.

Further research into faculty attitudes toward university-policy questions indicated that professors by a large margin favored larger salary increases with fewer additional benefits over more fringe benefits with smaller salary increases. This might again be an expression of confidence in their ability to manage their own affairs.

Night students, a major portion of the total student body at Metro University, received a relatively high evaluation from the faculty, with a mean of 5.49 on the evaluative scale. Similarly, emphasis on research received the faculty's endorsement, with an evaluative mean of 5.39.

On the other hand, extracurricular activities were lower on the scale. The concept "Metro Festival"—a controversial annual student event which has since been curtailed—received a faculty rating only slightly above the theoretically neutral point. Respondents viewed athletic scholarships, with an evaluative-scale mean of 3.99, just slightly below neutral.

❧ THE ERRING COLLEAGUE ❧

The responses to one of the most provocative questions in our study somewhat reflect faculty attitudes in several areas already discussed earlier, for example, attitudes toward the teaching profession and toward university policy. This question, which we asked in the pretest interview, reads, *If you were the president of a university and Charles Van Doren applied for a position as a faculty member, would you hire him?* Charles Van Doren is, of course, the professor from a large Eastern university who, after astounding television viewers by his seemingly incredible ability to answer difficult questions on a series of quiz programs, shocked the nation by admitting that he had received the answers in advance. When he was relieved of his teaching position, the academic community became involved in a lively discussion as to whether he should have been fired.

Among our respondents, 43 favored hiring Charles Van Doren, while 51 were against it. Twenty-five were without a crystallized opinion. About an equal number of reasons were given in favor of hiring him and against it. Among the largest number of reasons given for employing him were these two: An employer should take advantage of the fact that he was a good instructor (48), and since he had admitted his guilt, he should be given another chance (33). Surprisingly enough, 17 felt that anyone else would have done the same thing, and 16 believed he was a victim of circumstances and saw no moral issue involved since the quiz was off campus. On the other hand, some of those who were against hiring this key figure in the scandal gave these reasons: He was dishonest and immoral—a man, in short, who had disqualified himself as a college professor (40); he had displayed an unprofessional attitude, was unethical, and had no excuse for his action (18). Fifteen feared his hiring would be bad public relations and would harm the university's reputation, while 14 pointed to the fact that he would never gain the respect and trust of the students, and would even set a bad example for them.

From these data we may perhaps conclude that the professor views his colleague who errs ethically in the same harsh manner characteristic of other groups, such as the medical and legal professions. Yet, the Metro faculty appeared to be torn by the fact that Charles Van Doren was also an excellent instructor who, aside from his transgression, would make a most desirable addition to any teaching staff. Therefore, some of our respondents tried to rationalize hiring him in spite of his infraction.

FIVE

PROFESSORS AND INSTRUCTIONAL TELEVISION

In the preceding chapter, we used our data to present a general overview of the attitudes and value structure of the Metro University faculty. Having looked at their responses to a number of items which contribute to the school's social and intellectual climate, we are now ready to consider the focal point of our study, faculty attitudes toward instructional television (ITV).

✻ FACULTY RESISTANCE TO ITV ✻

On the basis of what we have presented, a prediction could undoubtedly be made about the attitude of the university professor toward ITV. His general reluctance to desert tried-and-true teaching methods, along with his firm belief that only through personal contact can the student be properly motivated, predict his reluctance to accept ITV as a vehicle for teaching. As a result, we should not be too surprised that virtually every educational institution which has attempted to use ITV in its curricula has encountered massive hostility on the part of its faculty, and, not infrequently, from its administration. As we pointed out in our introduction, one purpose of this research case history was to collect data during the course of the diffusion of an actual innovation that would more clearly pinpoint the extent and nature of this resistance.

The reader will recall that when we presented our respondents' ratings of teaching methods from the original questionnaire (see Table 3), television lectures were rated thirteenth of 14 items, with only teaching machines ranking lower. Students rated television lectures slightly higher, placing them eleventh. This fact may be a significant indication that students would be less hostile toward ITV if their attitudes were not considerably influenced by those of their teachers. McKeachie (1962) points out that ". . . one of the most interesting outcomes of the studies of student attitudes toward television instruction is that they tend to reflect those of the proctors in the viewing rooms" (p. 351). Undoubtedly, this is not the whole story. Other factors also seem to be responsible for student attitudes. A study by Evans, Wieland, and Moore (1961) concludes that "Negative attitudes toward television instruction may be less the result of experience in taking telecourses than of such factors as poor course performance. In other words, television as a medium of instruction may become an available whipping post because of its novelty for latent hostile attitudes arising from other factors in the college course situation" (p. 15). In any case, television lectures rank low among preferred teaching methods, as well as among learning methods.

Examining now the data elicited by the Osgood Semantic Differential, we can plot the direction, as well as the extent, of faculty resistance. Five ITV concepts from the original questionnaire are shown below, together with the mean of the responses on the evaluative scales:

	Item	Overall Mean (Evaluative Scale)
1.	Television instruction in introductory courses	4.02
2.	Straight television instruction for large classes	3.48
3.	Television instruction supplemented by small discussion sections for large classes	4.73
4.	Television instruction in advanced courses	3.57
5.	Myself conducting a television course	4.42

Even a cursory examination of these data reveals that the general reaction to these concepts was unfavorable on the evaluative scale when compared with other teaching concepts (see Table

69

1). In fact, only three of the five television concepts elicited evaluative-scale means of greater than the theoretical neutral point of 4.00. *Television supplemented by small discussion sections for large classes* elicited the highest evaluation among the ITV concepts. Attitudes toward this item may well have been influenced by the then prevailing pattern of telecourses at Metro, which utilized ITV for some of the introductory courses (for example, biology, psychology, political science, and trigonometry), with two television lectures per week and small discussion sections once a week. The indication here, however slight, is that involvement even in an indirect manner may alter attitudes. We will explore this in greater depth in a subsequent chapter on attitude change. Similarly, the second highest evaluative-scale mean was obtained when the concept "television course" was combined with the concept "myself," which probably raised it above the neutral point. Although basically opposed to ITV, the Metro professor seemed to feel that he would be capable of conducting a television course and, as a result, would enhance the value of television as an instructional device. By projecting himself into a television-teaching situation, he accordingly raised his opinion of the medium to a significant extent.

Having presented the extent of opposition to ITV among the Metro faculty, let us examine the more subjective responses to the open-end questions of the pro-ITV and anti-ITV groups. These responses were obtained by again using the quasi role-playing device (Evans, 1952), which we described earlier as a technique that instructs the respondent to imagine himself first opposed to, and then in favor of, a particular item—in this case, ITV. Actually, this item appeared in both the pretest and posttest interviews, but we will discuss the responses now without regard to the different frequency of occurrence in the two sets of data. (These frequency differences are analyzed in Chapter 7.)

Our respondents' strongest reason for opposing ITV centered around the lack of personal contact with students. They said that even if ITV reaches more students, what could a professor do about such problems in the viewing situation as distractions, a lack of intellectual atmosphere, or a lack of proper motivation? Would these not interfere with acquiring knowledge through television? A professor, they added, might become convinced that television lectures would reduce his teaching load and leave more time for research, but he could still oppose ITV because of the greater difficulty of teaching through the medium. Some felt that without feedback from students, controversial viewpoints expressed by the teacher might be misinterpreted. They pointed out that a teacher might find television acceptable for straight lecture presentations, particularly when he considers the advantage of being able to re-use good lectures and thereby present them to an even larger number of students; however, for the teaching of laboratory courses, he would find this method inferior. While some of our respondents admitted that ITV is economical, effective, and efficient (from the university's standpoint), they felt that an instructor might be justified in fearing it as an innovation which might even lead to widespread unemployment of classroom teachers.

As the interviewer moved from using the role-playing device to questioning the respondents as to how they actually felt and the reasons for their beliefs, the range of answers was considerable. A composite picture of these responses follows, again without particular concern for frequency counts or differences between pretest and posttest interviews.

Television in general: A small minority of our respondents expressed unqualifiedly favorable opinions about ITV. Some were merely indifferent, while others opposed it quite strongly. A small minority stated flatly that if its use should become widespread, they would quit teaching and go into research. In between were those who saw the medium as being useful for some subject-matter areas and highly advantageous if used in suitable places by certain individuals under certain circumstances. They saw a need, however, for further experimentation. This gave some indication that they

71

were at least willing to try ITV. Finally, a few appeared to be receptive to ITV only in the sense that they were in favor of experimenting with *anything* innovative.

ITV as a replacement for the classroom lecture: Again, in this category, acceptance, if any, was tempered by many qualifications. Our respondents might cautiously admit that a student body different from Metro's, one with more initiative to dig out information, might benefit and learn from ITV. They hastened to point out that not all courses lend themselves to television; as a matter of fact, they thought that the areas in which it could be used were very limited. ("You couldn't teach an entire course in political science on TV.") They could not, therefore, see it as a substitute for the classroom lecture. Some granted that some advantage might exist in using television as a supplement, but they felt that teacher and student must meet face to face during certain periods to thrash out the pros and cons of a subject. Combined at this time with recitation, television might be effective. It could also become a good study aid.

Ideal academic level for instructional television: None of our respondents suggested ITV for use in graduate instruction. Some disagreement arose as to whether it was desirable in basic courses, particularly at the freshman introductory level. Some felt it would be useful here; others thought it was undesirable for introductory courses and viewed with disfavor any television instruction for first-year students. Some felt that ITV might be useful for showing recent advances in science to the general public, for keeping the community informed, and for entertaining viewers. They envisioned ITV as a valuable tool for adult education, such as providing home-study courses in foreign languages.

ITV: What methods for what subjects? Here the range of responses was again very great. Some felt instructional television might be used in straight lecture courses where purely factual material was presented, while a number of others saw the possibility of presenting certain types of demonstrations, particularly in the natural sciences. But there was a strong feeling that while television

72

instruction might be helpful in some courses, it was not yet applicable to the respondent's particular area. Remarks made in this context included the following: "Art courses cannot be taught by TV until the color is improved." "One cannot teach history by this method." "Perhaps it could be used for music appreciation, but not for teaching theory and composition." "There would be little application of TV for engineering work, and it would not do for vocational-shop teaching."

Size of class: Responses in this category, though few in overall number, were fairly positive. For large classes, some respondents actually admitted that television might be better than lectures; they could see its potential for overcoming the obstacles that teachers often face in large lecture halls. As an alternative to limiting the number of students, instructional television might be preferable. But they felt it should be used only for large classes in certain courses; a good teacher in a small class they considered as the ideal.

Quality of course: The majority of respondents stated that instructional television has no real academic status. Its use might well lead to mass mediocrity. If it were any good, universities with greater prestige than Metro's would have adopted it. It is doubtful, they thought, that a truly superior university would use it. Furthermore, instruction on television could not be compared with classroom instruction; it would lower academic standards, commercialize education, and weaken it. A few felt that ITV would upgrade educational programs. Some, however, believed that television lectures might be superior to classroom instruction and that some well-known institutions were using this teaching method.

Professors' perceptions of student attitudes: Some interviewees were sure that students dislike taking televised courses. They reported that students feel they cannot get questions answered and that they resent the barriers which television lectures raise between themselves and the faculty. Among some of the respondents' reasons for disliking ITV were its many negative effects on learning. They felt that the student watching television at home or in the dormitory is exposed to the many distractions of non-classroom environments, relaxes too much, and does not take learning seriously. If the student fails, they pointed out, the instructor does not know whether the failure resulted from the student's not watching or not studying enough or, rather, because the presentation was inadequate. Then, too, television courses in such subjects as foreign languages make it difficult for the teacher to audit a student's oral performances. However, four of our respondents actually admitted that they thought very few students fail television courses, indicating that average grades in ITV courses are higher than—or at least equal to—those resulting from traditional classroom teaching.

Effects on the teacher and his profession: Some interviewees felt that because instructional television could reach a large number of students—among whom were those who might not be able to come to the university lecture hall itself—the method might help meet the "Communist challenge" to our technology, relieving the teacher shortage at least in part and meeting the needs of future increased enrollment. Some felt that while an ITV system is expensive in its introductory phase when it may be used only on a limited basis, as it becomes more widely used large savings could be made in the future by reducing costs per student. On the other hand, some believed that television lectures would require considerable preparation, making it difficult, if not impossible, for the professor teaching an ITV class to do justice to his other courses. He would have to make constant revisions of his lectures, the result being increased preparatory time. However, some felt that through ITV, both teacher and student could conserve time and energy. If, for example, students were unable to understand a particular lesson, it could easily be repeated.

Television teaching and classroom teaching the respondents saw as two completely different operations. They felt that television accentuates limitations in methods and puts considerable emphasis on the lecturer's personality, which must have certain qualifications that few possess. (One respondent remarked, "I wouldn't be a

74

good TV instructor," and another said, "Probably fine as long as I'm not involved.") They definitely felt that personal experience is the main factor, along with adequate training. As far as they were concerned, the good classroom teacher—the one who is enthusiastic and stimulating—should be doing television teaching. In fact, the school should use the best lecturers available for ITV courses.

Student-instructor contact: As we have already seen from the responses to the questions involving quasi role playing, this category drew the most critical evaluation of television as a teaching device. In none of the other areas did the professors speak so much with one voice. Here is a composite summary of what they said: "Interaction is lost; the student cannot express himself; he can't ask questions or express his opinion. Without student contact, I don't want to teach. Professors want to know their students; students need personal contact, because, after all, learning is a spiritual process of student-teacher relationship. It's better to have a poor instructor in the classroom than to have a good one on TV." Then, too, they felt that learning depends on the personal needs of students who have individual differences, deficiencies, and shortcomings, which television in the classroom cannot adequately meet.

By now the reader surely needs no further comments to grasp the strongly negative feelings of the Metro faculty toward ITV. Even when we include the moderately positive statements, the negative ones outnumber them two to one. This means that even the group which we arbitrarily labeled pro-ITV had many reservations about television teaching. This fact is important to keep in mind when we come to the discussion of the pro- and anti-ITV groups in the next chapter.

✽ ITV AND OTHER ATTITUDES ✽

To what extent are the above attitudes toward ITV necessarily interrelated with those that concern characteristics of the university climate—attitudes that we also examined in the research case history? This question was not only of theoretical interest to us, but it was also repeatedly voiced by administrators and faculty members in our discussions at the nine other universities, reported in Chapter 8. For example, many respondents in these later discussions felt that instructional-media innovations may not be typical of innovations in higher education and that attitudes toward ITV are unrelated to attitudes toward other innovations within the university.

The question of interrelatedness is one that cannot be answered easily. As we pointed out earlier, attitudes tend to cluster and belief systems tend to show considerable consistency. However, ample evidence indicates exceptions to this generalization. The consistency of attitude clusters appears to be relative rather than absolute, frequently permitting the existence of some isolated attitudes which are outside of, or even contradictory to, the individual's overall belief system.

One approach to finding an answer to this question is represented by our factor analysis of the 300 Osgood items from the initial questionnaire.[1] In general, these results supported our findings described earlier. From the factors we could identify two major patterns, one which we might label "pure ITV," that is, factors which showed an intrarelatedness of concepts in the ITV framework of attitudes. Here we found an indication that at least some professors were quite consistent in the manner in which they perceived, evaluated, and acted toward instructional television. In some cases these attitudes appeared to be relatively isolated or autonomous—that is, related to only very few other aspects of the academic community.

The second pattern which emerged from our factor analysis is one which we might label "ITV with non-ITV factors." This means that our respondents had clusters of attitudes which were not only related to ITV but also to their pre-established beliefs and feelings toward various aspects of the university climate in general. Here, attitudes toward ITV were related to other innovations, such

[1] This analysis was completed at the Survey Research Center, University of California at Berkeley.

as teaching machines, tuition increase, and honors and correspondence courses.

On the basis of these findings, we would question the assertion, often made by advocates of ITV, that the college professor has a nemesis-like conception of television which stands in isolation from his other attitudes. Our study would indicate to the contrary. On the other hand, a basis does indeed exist for suggesting that some professors may on occasion isolate and "see" ITV in a context of attitudes narrowly confined to television. Such professors are apparently neither reacting to it in terms of any attitudes which they held prior to their exposure to television teaching nor in terms of other attitudes which they currently hold. Some analysts of attitude structure have made similar theoretical observations about attitudes in general. For example, Rokeach (1960) refers to this phenomenon as the relative "isolation and differentiation" of attitudes or beliefs. In our study some individuals displayed a rather isolated array of attitudes related specifically to ITV, while others expressed attitudes toward ITV that were interrelated with different clusters of beliefs.

In the same vein as in our earlier discussion of this problem, Rokeach (1960) suggests that an isolated cluster of attitudes may sometimes reflect the "existence of logically contradictory beliefs within the belief system" (p. 36). As an example he cites the not uncommon attitude of "believing in freedom for all, but also believing that certain groups should be restricted." We observed a parallel to this type of isolation in our investigation, typified by such statements from our respondents as the following: "ITV is a fine instructional medium and should be encouraged for all to improve instruction, but not for my subject area"; and "ITV is the best means of teaching in the long run, but I would leave college teaching if I had to use it."

 SIX

PRO-ITV AND ANTI-ITV PROFESSORS

Thus far, our study has focused mainly on the nature and extent of attitudes directly or indirectly related to television as an instructional device in college teaching. We have used our data to present a composite picture of these attitude clusters without structuring them into a complete framework which could be identified as making up the personality of the pro- or anti-ITV professor. In this chapter we will present some data and interpretations which will create such personality images. We should like to emphasize, once again, that the professors we are about to create are "statistical men" or prototypes to which we will attribute extreme attitudes. Few if any of our respondents were literally in either of the extreme groups even in a statistical sense, that is, possessing all of the characteristics of the prototype. In fact, most of them fell in a group midway between the extreme polarities. For this reason an individual faculty member may display characteristics that we observed in both extreme groups or, possibly, none from either of them.

The reader will recall from our presentation of methods and procedures that we established the two opposed groups on the basis of our analyses of responses to the original questionnaire. The specific criterion for selecting the extremely favorable and extremely unfavorable groups was our respondents' attitudes toward the concept *Television instruction in*

78

large-enrollment introductory courses. This item appeared to evoke the most unqualified reactions to ITV, producing sufficiently large samples of responses measuring 7 and 6 points (favorable) and 1 and 2 points (unfavorable) on the *good-bad, weak-strong,* and *valuable-worthless* scales. On this basis, then, we selected the 55 pro-ITV and 65 anti-ITV subjects for our study. As we will see later, the validity of this criterion for selecting people was confirmed by other responses to related questions, particularly the open-end responses in the pretest and posttest interviews.

✹ THE PRO-ITV PROFESSOR ✹

What sort of person becomes an innovator or an adopter in a community in which considerable hostility is shown toward an innovation? This is one of the main questions that social psychologists and sociologists raise in the studies which we reviewed in Chapter 2. Obviously, an innovator or an adopter must have some characteristic attitudes which, if not causally related to his more favorable attitude toward certain innovations, at least coexist with them.

The results of our study at Metro University project some interesting images of the innovators in at least one such community confronted with a specific innovation. To explore this question in depth, we, of course, had to pinpoint in what ways the responses from the pro-ITV group differed from those of the anti-ITV group. To find these areas of disagreement, we applied the chi square test of statistical significance to the differences in response frequencies. Since this statistical method is commonly used in the behavioral sciences, we can simply say here that it is a means of determining whether a given distribution of values differs enough from those of another distribution to indicate the operation of non-chance factors. Such significance is denoted by various levels of confidence, that is, chance levels. In prevailing statistical practice, a minimum of .05 is required to denote an acceptable level of significance. Hence, when we show a difference between the two groups at a .01 level, it indicates that a significant probability exists that this is a charactcristic of both groups. On the other hand, when we show a difference at the .10 level, the chance of its being a real difference does not meet the generally accepted criterion of statistical significance. Actually, because small samples impose difficulties in yielding statistically significant results, we will report not only statistically significant differences but—in the exploratory spirit of our investigation—trends which may be interesting even if they are not important in the statistical sense.

Table 5 shows the items on which the pro-ITV group responded markedly higher than the anti-ITV group, as well as the levels at which these differences were statistically significant.

TABLE 5

94 ITEMS IN WHICH THE PRO-ITV GROUP RESPONDED SIGNIFICANTLY HIGHER THAN THE ANTI-ITV GROUP

Initial Questionnaire—Osgood Data

	Significance Levels			
Item	.01	.02	.05	.10
Metro Festival		Pleasant	Honest Valuable	Good
Athletic scholarships	Good Honest Fair Pleasant Valuable			
More fringe benefits with smaller salary increase	Good Pleasant	Smooth Fair	Strong	
Emphasis on research				Strong Valuable
Training in teaching methods for professors			Valuable	
Training in teaching methods for prospective professors			Fair	Active
Lecture method supplemented by small discussion section for large classes				Pleasant

80

Pro-ITV and Anti-ITV

	Significance Levels			
Item	.01	.02	.05	.10
Television instruction in introductory courses	All scales			
*Straight television instruction for large classes	9 scales out of 10			
Correspondence courses	Fair Strong	Smooth		Good Active Hard
*Television instruction supplemented by small discussion section for large classes	8 scales out of 10		Smooth	
*Television instruction in advanced courses	8 scales out of 10	Active		
Teaching machines	Honest Strong Valuable	Fair	Good	Fast
*Myself conducting a television course	7 scales out of 10			Active Fast
Myself conducting a small class		Strong		

Academic and Background Data

	Significance Levels			
Item	.01	.02	.05	.10
Teaching methods preferred:				
Class demonstration			x	
Field trips			x	
Motion pictures	x			
Supplementary TV viewing	x			
Teaching machines	x			
Television lectures	x			
Total number of various teaching methods selected was higher for pro-ITV group				x

* "Hard-Soft" not significant

RESISTANCE TO INNOVATION

Significance Levels

Item	.01	.02	.05	.10
Criteria for Evaluating Students:				
Attitude				x
Objective tests				x
Promptness in completing assignments				x
More pro-ITV professors have taught at more institutions		x		

Pre-Experimental Interview

Significance Levels

Item	.01	.02	.05	.10
Liked questionnaire		x		
Approved questionnaire	x			
Judges' overview ratings on questions 8–12 (all concerning teaching machines)	Favor			
Judges' overview ratings on questions 13–16 (imagine self strongly favoring ITV; imagine self strongly opposed to ITV; how you personally feel about ITV and why)	Favor			
Hire Van Doren?			Yes	
He was a good instructor				x
Summary of interview ratings	Tolerant Sophisti-cated			

* "Hard-Soft" not significant

Post-Experimental Interview

Significance Levels

Item	.01	.02	.05	.10
Number of miscellaneous advantages in using VTR* to improve teaching				x
Judges' overview ratings of questions 8 and 9 (personal feeling about ITV and why)	Favor			

* Video-tape recorder

Surveying the pattern of attitudes which the pro-ITV group displayed to a considerably greater extent than the anti-ITV group, we can make several generalizations. They were clearly less conservative, less traditionally oriented, and perhaps, in a way, less "scholarly" and "academic" in the narrow sense of the word. They tended to feel that the university climate can and should include some non-curricular or extracurricular activities, such as the "Metro Festival" and athletic scholarships, to assure a better athletic program for the school. Furthermore, their attitudes toward teaching and student evaluation also showed significant differences. A person in this group seemed somewhat less self-assured. Although he was, of course, willing to teach on television, the only other significant "myself" concept was teaching a small class. Method seemed more important to him than to his colleagues. Not only was he willing to receive more training, but he was also far more eager to experiment with various instructional methods, such as class demonstrations, field trips, motion pictures, television viewing, and even teaching machines and television lectures. Similarly, he reported that he evaluated student performance along more diverse lines, including such criteria as attitude, answers on objective tests, and promptness in completing assignments. Again, this may be some indication that less intellectual factors played a greater role in the pro-ITV group's view of the total university.

83

No one will be surprised that we found great differences between the pro-ITV and anti-ITV groups on the items "TV instruction in introductory courses," "Straight television for large classes," and "Television with discussion groups." As the table shows, all differences were in the predicted direction, a fact that provided us with a check on the validity of our criterion for selecting the two extreme groups. The pro-ITV respondents apparently felt that the greatest value of television would be in easing the teacher shortage, again an indication that pragmatic problems were of greater concern to them than to the opposing group. They also responded, in line with their concern for method, with a significantly greater number of miscellaneous advantages for the video-tape recorder to improve teaching. Significantly more of these instructors also liked and approved the original questionnaire than did their anti-ITV colleagues. In the interview situation, more of the pro-ITV group were judged to be tolerant and sophisticated and less hostile and bland. Thus, they appeared to be less opposed to instrusions into their own lives by others.

Perhaps one explanation for several of these results is the fact that the pro-ITV professors had taught at more institutions. Intuitively, we would hypothesize that exposure to a large number of different institutions would broaden an instructor's view of education. He would, of necessity, have gained greater flexibility from dealing with a variety of attitudes within different institutions and among diverse groups of colleagues. However, to belabor this fact too long would be misleading. As we pointed out earlier, some danger lies in assigning causal attributes to statistical relationships. Perhaps the pro-ITV professor, possessing greater flexibility and more willingness to experiment, is more likely to present himself to more institutions for employment, while the less flexible, more academically oriented, and possibly somewhat pedantic professor would rather stay "put," build his academic position, and not look to the other side of the fence, even if greener grass might be growing there.

Our data would tend to support the limited empirical findings available concerning the innovator or earlier-adopter personality. For example, Rogers (1962) points out that innovativeness (the degree to which an individual is relatively earlier in adopting an idea than the other members in a social system) is related to a modern (flexible) orientation rather than to a traditional (rigid) one. He goes on to note that observers have found that venturesomeness is almost an obsession with innovators.

To round out the image of the pro-ITV instructor, we must look at some of the items on which he scored significantly lower than his colleagues. In a way, these negatively weighted items may be as characteristic of his personality as those to which he responded positively. Apparently, he felt less positive about the concept "night students" than his anti-ITV colleague. On the whole, these more mature students, who are already involved in a profession or occupation, tend to contribute little to the non-academic aspects of a university. In the jargon of the college campus, they are said to have no "school spirit." They are, on the other hand, known for the seriousness with which they approach their education, wanting to get the maximum out of every available hour—in short, they want to get their tuition money's worth. They may have little patience with an instructor who experiments, feeling that they lack time for such experimentation since they want to get down to facts in the shortest possible time. Generally, they have no interest in extracurricular activities like festivals or athletics. As we will see, these may be characteristics which impressed the anti-ITV respondents more favorably than their colleagues.

✹ THE ANTI-ITV PROFESSOR ✹

As we move now from one end of the spectrum to the other, the data shown in Table 6 provide us with the quite different image of the anti-ITV professor. In contrast to the pro-ITV group, the anti-ITV respondents were academically oriented. To them the traditional academic values of the university discussed in a preceding chapter were central to their outlook. They viewed with

TABLE 6

30 ITEMS IN WHICH THE ANTI-ITV GROUP RESPONDED SIGNIFICANTLY HIGHER THAN THE PRO-ITV GROUP

Initial Questionnaire—Osgood Data

Item	Significance Levels			
	.01	.02	.05	.10
Night students				x
Additional tuition increase			Un-pleasant	
Larger salary increase with fewer additional fringe benefits	Pleasant Hard Valuable		Good Honest	Fair Strong
Becoming a state university	Active Fair		Good Honest Valuable	Strong Pleasant
Admitting qualified Negroes	Active Strong	Fair	Good Smooth	
Straight lecture method		Pleasant		
Answering students' questions in large classes	Good			
Myself conducting a lecture course	Good			
Myself conducting a large class				Good

Academic and Background Data

Item	Significance Levels			
	.01	.02	.05	.10
Criteria for evaluating students: spelling				x

Pre-Experimental Interview

Item	Significance Levels			
	.01	.02	.05	.10
Heavier teaching load			x	

86

Significance Levels

Item	.01	.02	.05	.10
Hire Van Doren?			Against	
He had unprofessional . . . . Closely				
attitude, was unethical,				approached
dishonest, immoral				this level
Number of miscellaneous				
disadvantages to ITV		x		

In response to the specific questions "How do you personally feel about television?" and "Why?" the anti-ITV group gave the following answers significantly more often that did the pro-ITV group:

Significance Levels

Item	.01	.02	.05	.10
Television courses give bad results	x			
Interpersonal relationships are left out		x		

In response to the specific questions "How do you personally feel about television?" and "Why?" the pro-ITV group gave the following answers significantly more often than the anti-ITV group:

Significance Levels

Item	.01	.02	.05	.10
General statements:				
"TV good"	x			
"Aid teacher shortage"	x			

considerable indifference, or even hostility, those items which were peripheral to the university as they perceived it. Some evidence shows that they tended to rationalize hostility toward such peripheral items by counter-relating them to their academic position and academic preoccupation.

As mentioned earlier, the one overall characteristic which Rogers hypothesizes as the mark of the laggard, or the last person to adopt an innovation, is tradition. The laggard's reference point is in the past. He makes his decisions on the basis of what previous generations have done. He tends to be frankly suspicious of innovations and innovators. The prototype of the anti-ITV professor fits this model rather well. His major preoccupation is with the traditional approach to instruction, as indicated by his significantly higher evaluations of such concepts as "Straight lecture method" and "Answering students' questions in large classes." His self-image is one of adequacy, at least within his limited field of academic endeavor, as shown by his significantly higher evaluation of the array of concepts prefaced by "Myself conducting." We may also view this as further verification of the "professionalistic" disposition of the anti-ITV professor.

A further indication of inconsistency of attitudes toward diverse innovations emerged in the anti-ITV group's response to the concept "The university becoming a state university." Perception of this change appeared to be independent of members' perception of the technical innovation. If we accept Rogers' postulate (1962) that "Perception [of an innovation] is a function of the situational fields within which the individual operates" (p. 303), we can relate the anti-ITV group's favorable responses to this conception to their pre-eminent concern with the academic aspects of their existence. Perhaps members felt that Metro as a state university would possess more academic prestige and attract more applicants, thus providing more opportunity to select a better qualified student body. Miles (1964) describes such innovations as non-disturbing, since they can be fitted easily into the individual's existing value structure.

As Evans (1952) in his discussion of the operation of rationalization could have predicted, the quasi role-playing technique of measuring attitudes resulted in the anti-ITV professor's being able to state a significantly larger number of different disadvantages of ITV than his pro-ITV colleague. When asked to give reasons why he personally opposed ITV, he pointed much more often to the fact that television courses give bad results and that interpersonal relationships are left out. However, while apparently revealing more concern with interpersonal relationships through some responses, he tended to use fewer criteria in evaluating students. Furthermore, the single yardstick which he preferred to use more often here than the pro-ITV professor was the pedantic criterion of spelling. In part, his higher valuation of this subject may have been conditioned by his "psychological field," since his academic specialty tended to be more central to the traditional university areas, where we may generally assume more preoccupation with writing style as such.

Why did the anti-ITV respondents seem more interested in "Larger salary increase with fewer additional fringe benefits"? Again, several explanations are possible. Attitudes toward the concept may be related to this group's self-image. To the instructor who has high confidence in his own judgment and who adheres to more traditional values, fringe benefits may appear to be innovations aimed at reducing his role in deciding how to allocate his income. However, our anti-ITV professor may simply have selectively responded to the first part of this concept, "larger salary increase." If the latter is the case, we might suspect that this group received less salary than our pro-ITV respondents. Since university policy made it impossible in the present study to obtain professors' individual salaries, we were unable to obtain data confirming or denying such a hypothesis. However, indirect supporting data might be deduced from our finding that our anti-ITV respondents carried heavier teaching loads than their pro-ITV counterparts. Typically in American universities, a negative correlation exists between salary and the number of teaching hours. Thus, professors who have large teaching loads are those whose names appear at the lower end of the pay scale. Admittedly, such a deduction from our data is questionable, but it does suggest one generalization from other studies (Rogers, for example), that earlier adopters have a more favorable financial position than late adopters.

Briefly recapping our findings, we may picture the pro-ITV professor as being more adventuresome, flexible, and mobile in his thinking and teaching. His concern is not limited to the narrowly defined academic aspects of the university; rather, he tends to see the university as a social as well as academic community. As far as the academic aspects of his existence are concerned, he is far more willing to experiment with new methods and techniques than his anti-ITV colleague. However, in regard to innovations which affect the social aspects of the university, he may be less willing to support change. In any case, he is interested in a wide range of questions which transcend the traditional university boundaries.

At the opposite extreme of the continuum, we find that the anti-ITV professor is narrowly focused on questions and events which revolve around the traditional academic framework. The acceptance or rejection of any concept depends, for him, on the way in which it fits into his academically ordered world. He perceives himself as being highly competent in his chosen profession, and thus he spends more time doing what he thinks he does best —teaching by traditional methods. He sees as the greatest threat those forces within his environment which might "dilute" the academic aspects of the university, or alter his role within it.

Of course, most of our respondents were not clearly either pro- or anti-ITV in all areas. In other words, most of the population studied favored ITV in some ways and in some ways opposed it, while others, perhaps, were indifferent toward it. However, as investigations have shown in most American universities, professors as a group are inclined to be opposed to the use of television instruction, rather than in favor of it. If we place pro- and anti-ITV attitudes along a spectrum, it is likely that most of our population, which was, of course, at least moderately anti-ITV, could *not* be considered to possess many of the qualities which at least statistically appeared to characterize our *extreme* anti-ITV group. Likewise, few of the professors who were moderately pro-ITV would possess many of the qualities which at least statistically appeared to characterize our extreme pro-ITV group. This should be made clear since, as we indicated earlier, some faculty members, who themselves were, perhaps, at least moderately opposed to ITV, became defensive upon reading a preliminary report of our research case history (Evans *et al.,* 1963). They may have become

90

defensive because they could not actually apply many of the qualities of our statistical anti-ITV prototype to themselves, thus incorrectly interpreting the meaning of such prototypes.

One of the most difficult tasks of a psychological investigator in a study utilizing such a select and rarely studied population as college professors is to communicate the ethics involved in such research. For example, in our research case history, we have not identified individuals and departments. Even the questions we chose to use may appear to some to reflect a bias on our part. In fact, some of the Metro faculty felt that our inclusion of an item relating to the number of papers each respondent had published implied that we were somehow emphasizing the importance of publishing as against good teaching. Others felt that our studying reactions to ITV of necessity meant that we were advocating its use.

We trust our use of prototypes of the extreme anti- and pro-ITV professors is judged from the objective perspective that we have tried to maintain throughout the present report. Our only purpose in such a comparison is to explore extreme reactions to one controversial innovation in the hope that this will help us generate more hypotheses about the social psychology of innovation in the American university. In fact, even the belief that innovation in general is necessarily good and resistance to innovation in general is necessarily bad would be an inappropriate bias for an investigator in this field.

With the aid of the prototypes we have introduced, we hope that we have suggested at least one approach to bringing a psychological level of analysis to innovation research at the university. Now we will look at some of the theoretical implications of our findings and, most especially, discuss the need for further research that uses more refined techniques to measure underlying psychological factors. Though carefully constructed, our techniques, in many ways, lacked sufficient sensitivity to produce data which would make reasonably broad predictions possible for individual or group behavior. However, our data do give us some provocative insights into personality and receptivity to innovation; these may suggest techniques which would help the researcher in higher education to understand and predict both innovative behavior and behavior that resists innovation.

❧ THEORY AND ITV PROTOTYPES ❧

Although the tendency of sociologists and cultural anthropologists has been to explain the range of attitudes toward innovation by analyzing a society and the individual's role merely as a component of it, we feel that a more psychologically directed insight into the person within a social system would provide an added dimension of understanding which could contribute significantly to whether an innovation will be accepted or rejected. This understanding could be achieved by probing more deeply into an individual's frame of reference, his values, and attitudes with respect to a particular innovation proposed for a university. It would require two further steps: first, to ferret out from the many personality attributes which show some possible relationship to the degree of individual acceptance of an innovation, those which appear most likely to bear a causal relationship; and, second, to design the methods and techniques necessary for more refined measurements of such personality traits, which the investigator can then utilize in more extensive and controlled investigations.

❧ THE COSMOPOLITE-LOCALITE DIMENSION ❧

An example of the problems that innovation theory encounters by ignoring psychological factors will illustrate the possible limitations of many sociological approaches, which sometimes appear to use simple behavioral descriptions to indicate psychological processes. Rogers reports a study by Ryan and Gross in which they found a positive relationship between the time a farmer took to adopt hybrid seed and the number of trips he made outside a small Iowa farming community to Des Moines. Rogers uses this study to show how such an empirically derived hypothesis tested operationally can be used to support a more general hypothesis which states that *innovativeness* varies directly with *cosmopolitanism*. (Leaving one's own environment regularly apparently indicates that one is relatively cosmopolite.) However, such a simple operational measure may not be an adequate one for a general theory. There is nothing inherent in going to Des Moines that changes the farmer's attitude toward hybrid corn. We need to know those factors involved in traveling to Des Moines which shape his attitude. There are several possibilities. On the way to Des Moines, he may observe that the fields of corn look better than his own and then note the brand of corn, a hybrid type advertised along the road. He may stop six miles outside the city limits to visit the experimental farm where Henry Wallace developed hybrid corn. His trips to Des Moines may even include visits to the Farmers' Institute where experts present many new innovations. On the other hand, he could quite conceivably make many trips to the city without modifying any of his attitudes toward hybrid corn. Conversely, the farmer who rarely travels to Des Moines may actually emerge as an innovator with a high degree of cosmopolitanism. He may listen regularly to farm programs broadcast by various radio and television stations and he may subscribe to and regularly read the *Des Moines Register,* a daily paper which prominently features farm news. Obviously, then, the number of trips a farmer makes to Des Moines would provide at most only a very gross index for measuring how much of a cosmopolite or a localite an individual is.

Our own study indicates the danger of taking similar superficial, and possibly spurious, relationships too seriously. For example, we found a positive relationship between the number of institutions at which each respondent had taught prior to coming to Metro and his favorable attitude toward ITV.[1] But as we pointed

---

[1] Miles (1964) similarly speculates that the teacher who is innovative in his field has worked in several different school systems.

93

out when we reported these data, many reasons may exist for such a correlation that need not signal a causal relationship at all.

Careful analysis of our findings—together with the empirical data of the few other studies in this area and our own informal data which we will report in Chapter 8—has, however, made one fact clear to us: One of the basic premises of innovation research, that innovativeness varies directly with cosmopolitanism and inversely with "localiteness," does represent a most promising area for further research in the social psychology of innovation in higher education. On the basis of a number of criteria, our data show that the professor who is receptive to new ideas from outside the social system represented by the university tends to look upon ITV more favorably than the professor whose orientation is perhaps too narrowly focused upon his own academic community.

We would suggest the development of a specific technique for measuring the psychological aspects of the cosmopolite-localite continuum. However, even without a specific study of this factor, we decided to include in our study some of the variables derived from our present research which we feel may help to develop a means for measuring this kind of behavior in the university faculty.

Seemingly, a cosmopolite individual must have channels reaching beyond his particular social system in order to receive new ideas, which frequently—and in some systems exclusively—come from the outside. This appears to be particularly important in educational systems because of the relative lack of change agents, who in some environments serve to introduce new ideas. We might include, then, some operational factors in our measuring device that we could weigh fairly easily. The frequency of attendance at regional and national meetings of professional societies, the number of professional and academic journals received, and the nature and amount of community involvement might provide a partial picture of the instructor's cosmopolitanism. But of even greater importance would be an index of the meaning which these explicit behaviors have for the individual professor. Does he see professional meetings as a true opportunity for acquiring information which will guide

94

his university life and stimulate him to new research? Or does he view these meetings as an opportunity to increase his status, to find support from kindred souls, and to strengthen his narrow academic outlook? Anyone who has attended professional meetings can attest to the fact that they can easily serve the latter purposes. If a professor subscribes to professional journals, we would need to know how he tends to use the information he gains from them. If he sees journals as a vital part of his continuing education, providing him with the latest information in his field which can alter both the content and method of his teaching, then they could be a valid means for measuring the degree of his cosmopolitanism and thereby help to predict how innovative he can be. In some instances, however, the professor who subscribes to journals may not read them at all, while the non-subscriber may borrow his colleague's copies or take them out from the library.

Our findings also lead us to suspect that significant individual differences exist in the ways in which college professors perceive the university as a whole. A refinement of our technique for measuring attitudes toward non-academic, even non-university, activities might yield highly predictive factors.

We may reasonably suspect that the cosmopolite professor's outside references provide him with a perspective of the university which is unavailable to the instructor who is a localite. While the latter can see the university only from inside the system itself— and often only from within his own discipline—the former, in a sense, can look from the outside in. This perspective may lead the cosmopolite to be more sensitive to the overall needs of the university community, while the localite tends to be concerned primarily with its academic development, frequently restricted to his field. The information channels open to the cosmopolite may, furthermore, influence his manner of teaching and methods of evaluating students. Thus, the significantly more favorable attitude toward field trips, motion pictures, and other non-conventional teaching devices, including ITV, may be the result, in part, of the pro-ITV instructor's cosmopolitanism. Similarly, his favoring of

95

promptness in completing assignments and student attitudes as evaluative criteria may well be values which are more related to his reference groups outside the university, while insistence on correct spelling may be more indicative of the academically centered orientation of the localite.

Greater communication with sources outside the university may also affect the way in which the innovator views himself and determines what poses a potential threat to him and the values he holds. Because he has greater knowledge of the community around the university and frequently relates to it, he is less afraid of exposing himself to it than the localite. Hence, we would expect that he would be less concerned over increased interrelationships between the university and the community. Specifically, he may feel less fearful than the localite in having to teach over an ITV station for the community at large. In all likelihood he is more open about his abilities and feels less need to be secretive about his knowledge and teaching methods. We may note here, parenthetically, in the quite different setting of industrial firms that Carter and Williams (1957) report that technical progressiveness was indicated by— among other factors—the worldwide travel of company executives and a lack of secretiveness with plant visitors.

Another interesting aspect of the problem which will require further investigation, possibly with a technique that measures the cosmopolite-localite factor, is the apparent clustering of individuals with one orientation in certain instructional fields. Is a cosmopolite orientation required or, at least, desirable in certain disciplines and less important or even undesirable in others? Again, we feel it stands to reason that those who teach engineering, technology, and communication must be in touch with the "outside" to keep up with developments. But should not the same be expected of those who teach the social and natural sciences?

At this point in our discussion, we encounter one of the major issues confronting higher education today. An ever increasing number of fingers are being pointed at the ineffectiveness of the humanities, the social sciences, and, to some extent, even the physical sciences to equip the student with the tools which make it possible for him to come to grips with the complexities of the twentieth century. Jacob (1957) provides an interesting review of those studies which show the ineffectiveness of one of these areas, the social sciences. He points out that effectiveness as measured by the changes in the values and attitudes of students is low—particularly in those institutions where only classroom instruction is offered. Among the innovations which he indicates would contribute to increased meaningfulness of course material to the student are laboratory-practice experiences, which—for the social sciences at least—mean involvement of the student (and teacher) in off-campus activities. He goes on to say that "Vicarious experience does not deliver the punch, even though 'role-playing' techniques in the classroom, and the analysis of challenging case studies and problem situations, do arouse more interest in the course" (p. 98).

In other words, changes in our current teaching methods require major innovations which ought to permeate all academic areas, not just those which are more peripheral to the university system to begin with and which by their nature are more dependent on the constant change characteristic of the technological developments in the community at large.

An example showing some broader implications of this problem is the situation that arose at the University of California at Berkeley during 1965 and 1966. Here much interest was focused on the psychological distance which had developed between professor and student. The protest movement at that school may, at least in part, have reflected students' hostility toward the increasingly impersonal pattern in their relationships with professors. This is an interesting example of the way in which the cosmopolite-localite dimension may be one factor affecting the social climate at a university.

Possibly as the number of cosmopolites increases at a university, faculty interest in teaching per se declines and the psychological distance between professors and students increases. The cosmopolite's reference groups increasingly envelop members of his own profession at large, national institutions and even society at large, while his immediate concern with his own students and interest in his local teaching role decline.[2]

The attacks against the "multiversity" at Berkeley, of which former president Clark Kerr bore the brunt, may have been partially rooted in this dilemma.

Thus, while the cosmopolite is more likely to tolerate or even promote innovations than his localite colleague, the latter may foster a closer association with his students, which reduces the psychological distance between professor and student. Here we can clearly see that although the identification of our prototype cosmopolite with the outside community may be responsible for his innovative behavior, it may be less desirable than a pattern of professional behavior which reflects constructive characteristics of both cosmopolite and localite orientations.

[2] The question of what might be the proper division of a professor's time and commitment among teaching, research, administration, public service, and private professional practice was explicitly raised by the Berkeley Academic Senate (University of California, 1965).

SEVEN

CHANGES IN ATTITUDE TOWARD INNOVATION

Our discussion in the preceding chapters may have given the erroneous impression that once an individual's attitudes are formed, they become inflexible and unchanging. For our purposes we needed to "fix" our hypothetical attitude clusters so that we could examine and analyze them. The actual fact, however, is that an individual's attitudes toward a particular object in his environment can and frequently do change. Just as individual species must make physical adjustments to their environment to survive physically, human beings, according to most behavioral scientists, must also make adjustments in their attitudes to survive social psychologically. Therefore, unless we want to live in partial or total social isolation, we are, from time to time, pressured to change certain of our outlooks. The extent of such changes, the speed with which they occur, and the discomfort we undergo while making such alterations depend partly on the forces in our social environment and partly on the degree to which the changing attitude is related to other clusters of attitudes which the individual holds.

The reader will recall from the chapter describing the purpose and methods of our research case history that one aspect of the present investigation became a field demonstration of the dynamics of attitude change. Before we present the empirical data of this part of our study, we might profitably look at some of the theories of attitude modification in general and, in a more detailed manner, examine the one which we selected to serve as a basis for our research.

❧ *THEORIES OF ATTITUDE CHANGE* ❧

The most widely discussed attitude theories in the contemporary literature of social psychology postulate that an individual's attitude constellation strives to maintain a balance, an equilibrium, or at least a tendency toward such a state, which is sometimes called homeostasis. This homeostatic model has its origin in physiology, where it has been used to describe the maintenance of constancy of relations in the bodily processes, for example, maintenance of body temperature, regardless of environmental temperature. The assumption is that any departure from the equilibrium sets in motion activities which tend to restore it. Are the dynamics of our attitudes analogous to this physiological model? A considerable amount of convincing empirical evidence shows that such a model is indeed applicable to certain social psychological phenomena, particularly an individual's affective cognitions, that is, his beliefs or feelings about a person or object which are an important component of his attitude toward them. A number of theories have been constructed, all representing variations on the same theme. They generally postulate that a state of equilibrium or balance exists in a belief system, so that the related elements within this framework are made up of non-contradictory items existing in harmony with each other; each, in short, is compatible with all of the others.

Perhaps we can best illustrate this postulate by again considering a set of beliefs which have a contradictory relationship. An individual may say, "I believe in freedom of the press; not all the news is fit to print; I favor some censorship of newspapers." According to the various balance theories, an unbalanced attitude or belief system tends to shift toward regaining an equilibrium. Thus, in the above case, the individual may end up approving of freedom of the press only within the boundaries of what he thinks is printable, or he may come to feel that censorship is too high a price to

100

pay just to eliminate an occasional item beyond that boundary.

Heider (1946) is considered by some to be the father of modern consistency or "balance" theory in psychology. He provides a detailed account of the phenomenology of relationships between individuals. He postulates a cognitive system made up of three components: the person himself, another individual, and an additional social object. Each of these cognitions could have positive or negative values or signs. A state of balance is achieved when the three values are either all positive or when two are negative. As an example, let us assume that we have a dislike for Orthovians (a non-existent ethnic group). A person whom we like also dislikes Orthovians. Here, our triadic cognitive system has two negative components and one positive component and is, therefore, in balance. Now let us assume that our friend likes Orthovians and acts accordingly; now the system is out of balance. In the struggle for equilibrium, either of two components must be changed. Either we must change our feelings about our friend or alter our attitude toward Orthovians.

Newcomb (1953) states a similar formulation in his theory of symmetry. His important contribution to this theoretical framework is the postulate that the negative or positive relations between cognitive events may also vary in intensity. Thus, he holds that the symmetry of a system requires not only identical signs but, furthermore, is dependent on equality of intensity.

Osgood and Tannenbaum (1955) later expanded this theoretical system. Referring to the equilibrium state of a cognitive system as "congruity," these investigators hold that the interactions of cognitive events are such that they modify each other's valences and intensities toward congruity with each other. The degree of such modification is inversely proportional to the original intensity of the isolated events prior to becoming related. According to their formulation, beliefs may have valences of zero or degrees of positive or negative intensity. Congruity is achieved when signs are all zero, or two are negative, and the intensities are equal. Using our earlier example, we might have a very strong positive affect related to our

101

friend. His slight positive affect for Orthovians will only slightly modify our feelings toward him, or toward Orthovians. If, on the other hand, he feels strongly positive toward them, then the modification of our belief system must be greater. We must either alter our strongly positive feeling toward our friend or drastically reappraise our negative attitude toward Orthovians.

For our research case history we decided to use what is perhaps the most general of the balance theories—the one that Festinger (1957) outlines in his *Theory of Cognitive Dissonance*—as the theoretical basis for the experimental aspect of our investigation. Again, Festinger's formulations are similar to those we have just described. As he himself points out, in respect to his substitution of the word "consonant" for "balanced" and "dissonant" for "imbalanced," Heider's theoretical considerations—as far as they go—are not unlike his own. Similarly, he points out that Osgood's and Tannenbaum's "principle of congruity" is not unlike his principle of consonance, "incongruity" being similar to the concept of dissonance. In his own words in his 1957 book, Festinger formulates his balance theory as follows: "There is pressure to produce consonant relations among cognitions and to avoid and reduce dissonance" (p. 9).

The most significant contribution that Festinger's theory of cognitive dissonance makes to balance theory in general is the manner in which it serves to broaden the theoretical base and to make it applicable to a variety of phenomena in social psychology. An important theoretical extension of this kind exists in the fact that dissonance theory links attitudes with overt behavior by stating the conditions prerequisite for the correspondence of attitudes and behavior. Normally, Festinger points out, an individual's opinions and attitudes tend to form clusters which are internally consistent, and his actions tend to be equally consistent with what he believes. What happens when inconsistencies occur may best be shown by quoting three points from Festinger (1957) which summarize his basic theory:

1. There may exist dissonant or "nonfitting" relations among cognitive elements,
2. The existence of dissonance gives rise to pressures to reduce the dissonance and to avoid increases in dissonance, and
3. Manifestations of the operation of these pressures include behavior changes of cognition, and circumspect exposure to new information and new opinion (p. 31).

Thus, Festinger's dissonance theory can interpret a variety of phenomena of interest to the behavioral scientist. Many of these, however, can also be interpreted by means of other theories. The phenomena which appear to be most accountable in terms of this theory, and perhaps uniquely so, are those which surround the consequences following an individual's choice between two or more mutually exclusive alternatives. Since his commitment to one of the alternatives also means a rejection of the other(s) and since both undoubtedly have some positive and some negative elements for him, dissonance is an almost inevitable consequence of such a decision. Since Festinger's theory holds that such dissonance leads to efforts to reduce it, in a number of ways the individual would augment the positive values of the chosen alternative(s) and similarly increase the negative aspects of the one(s) he rejected.

When an individual commits himself to behave in a manner inconsistent with his attitudes or beliefs, we have another situation which creates dissonance. Again, Festinger's theory can provide us with an interpretation of the resulting phenomena. He calls this situation, in which an individual decides to behave in a manner contrary to his beliefs or publicly expresses an opinion contrary to his private opinion, a *forced-compliance* situation. According to him, such forced compliance occurs generally only when the pressure to comply is accompanied by an offer of a reward for compliance or a threat of punishment for non-compliance. Again, dissonance is to some degree an inevitable consequence of a forced-compliance situation. The pressure to reduce such dissonance following compliance is a function of its magnitude, which, in turn, is a function of the relative importance of the elements forcing compliance. If the reward (or punishment) which compels an individual to act contrary to his privately held opinion is so great as to be grossly out of proportion to his opinion, dissonance will be minimal and, hence, the pressure to change his opinion will be equally small. As Festinger points out, a million dollars offered to a person in return for stating a positive opinion about comic books, to which he is opposed, will give rise to little dissonance. On the other hand, if the reward or punishment is just barely strong enough to persuade the person to act contrary to his belief, dissonance will be maximal and, therefore, attitude change should be greatest.

Festinger and Carlsmith (1959) report putting this aspect of dissonance theory to an empirical test. In a rather ingeniously designed experiment, they found that when subjects were paid a dollar to describe a boring task to someone else as interesting, they tended to persuade themselves that the task really was interesting and enjoyable. Other subjects, however, who were paid 20 dollars to conduct the same experiment were far less likely to change their privately held opinions. These results confirm the theory. Specifically, they show that if a person is forced to improvise a speech supporting a point of view with which he disagrees, his private opinion moves toward the position he advocates in the speech, provided the reward is great enough to elicit such expression and yet not so high as to eliminate the resulting dissonance.

The experimental phase of our investigation at Metro became a further test of this aspect of Festinger's theory. Instead of using verbal techniques, which are rather *abstract,* simulated involvement, or role playing, our investigation made an effort to involve participants in a real-life situation. The subjects who participated in this operational phase of our study were physically and psychologically involved in a forced-compliance situation, in which they were not artificially isolated in an "experimental climate." Our experiment in effect became a real-life test of dissonance theory as articulated by Festinger and Carlsmith (1959): "If a person is induced to do or say something which is contrary to his private opinion, there will be a tendency for him to change his opinion so as to bring it into correspondence with what he had done or said. The larger the pressure used to elicit the overt behavior (beyond the minimum needed to elicit it) the weaker the above mentioned tendency" (pp. 209–210).

❧ THE FORCED-COMPLIANCE EFFECT ❧

In the experimental phase of our investigation, we sought the answer to this question: As a theoretical exploration of the dynamics of attitude change, to what degree can a forced-compliance situation—as defined by Festinger and consisting of an ego-involving participation in instructional television—modify faculty attitudes toward ITV? Aside from our investigation of dissonance theory, it seemed incidentally to be interesting to determine what promise the video-tape recorder, as used by a participating faculty in the above situation, holds as a device for improving teaching.

Although our experimental design was in many ways similar to that which Festinger and Carlsmith employed, it differed significantly from theirs in some respects. Most important among these was that our forced-compliance situation was far more "real" than the laboratory setting which they used. The fact that of their 71 subjects 11 admitted they suspected that the forced compliance was not authentic indicates the drawback of laboratory-setting experiments in social psychology.

On the other hand, our experimental design suffered from this disadvantage: We were able to collect data for only a small number of experimental subjects, primarily because of economic restrictions. As reward for their participation, our subjects in the experimental phase, in addition to receiving their regular salaries, had the choice of either being relieved of some of their teaching load or of receiving compensation for overtime work in return for their participation. Our reward situation appeared to meet Festinger's and Carlsmith's criterion for predicting the greatest amount of attitude change, that is, a reward just high enough to produce

105

behavior which might be contrary to privately held opinion. However, an empirical verification of this with the situation and subjects involved would obviously have been difficult.

❧ SUBJECTS AND PROCEDURE ❧

The reader has already become acquainted with some of the operational procedures used in the present experiment. However, a brief review of the major steps leading up to the experimental phase may be helpful.

Subjects: On the basis of the responses to our original questionnaire (N = 319), we established two antipodal groups: (1) *pro-ITV*—individuals who responded most favorably to instructional television (N = 55); and (2) *anti-ITV*—individuals who responded most unfavorably to instructional television (N = 65). Among these 120 subjects were the 20 faculty members representing two departments in the College of Arts and Sciences (Departments "A" and "B"). These two departments, which we had sounded out earlier, had rejected official overtures to use television in their required introductory courses with large enrollments. These 20 faculty members were selected to participate in the natural field-setting experiment and, for purposes of this phase of our study, were labeled "EXP-ITV." Although their previous collective behavior reflected resistance, individually they were judged to be divided almost equally into pro-ITV, anti-ITV, and neutral-ITV groups on the basis of the initial questionnaire and the pretest interview. This division made them an ideal sample for an experimental study of attitude modification. Since all 120 subjects participated in the pretest and posttest interviews, the remaining 100 members served as a control group for the experimental phase between the pretest and posttest interviews.

After completion of the pretest interviews, given to both the control and experimental subjects, each person in the EXP-ITV group was asked to prepare, produce, and participate in at least one 45-minute presentation to be recorded on a video-tape recorder. As mentioned earlier, this device is similar to the familiar audio-tape recorders, providing immediate playback and erasure features for both the audio and visual components. It appeared to be the logical and ideal instrument for use in this study, because the investigators felt that it afforded the greatest self-improvement possibilities for instruction inherent in any medium in the history of education. After completion of these tapes, the participant was then asked to examine and react to the tape produced.

In addition to these efforts and as a means of increasing commitment to the task, all members of each of the two "experimental" departments were asked to collaborate in the production of several video tapes, which represented a cooperative effort.

EXP-ITV subjects were offered consultation, ITV reports, books, pamphlets, and other ITV information by the investigators. Basically, however, the planning and evaluation of each person's video-tape presentation was left entirely up to him. We had earlier postulated that this participation would produce the high degree of ego-involvement that we needed in our investigation; on the basis of the results, such appeared to be the case. Subsequently, few of the instructors requested assistance from our research staff to any appreciable degree. As a matter of fact, when participants actively sought detailed direction, our project staff simply emphasized that it did not want to give anything but general assistance. In order to fulfill the theoretical foundation of our study, we felt that the participants should be left to their own devices as much as possible.

The television production coordinator, a member of our project team who assisted faculty members in producing their tapes, provided a detailed written report on the quality of each tape and the verbal and non-verbal behavior of each participant "on camera." As mentioned earlier, the posttest interview then followed for each professor.

Finally, each experimental subject was asked to write a report on his experience and his opinion of the video-tape recorder as a device for improving teaching.

This descriptive summary of our subjects and experimental

107

procedure shows that our participants were not literally "forced" to take part in the experimental phase of the study, as was the case in Festinger's and Carlsmith's study in which students were required to participate in the experiment as part of a course in introductory psychology. Yet, in a more subtle way, our subjects' compliance could be conceived of as "forced" as defined by Festinger and Aronson (1960), even though there was the alternative to not participate. Once departments "A" and "B" had committed themselves as a whole to participation, we correctly assumed that subtle or direct intragroup pressures would be exerted upon the individual participant to meet departmental responsibilities. Finally, subsidization received by each participating faculty member in a sense made him a paid consultant, a role quite similar to Festinger's and Carlsmith's paid assistants.

The experimental design reviewed in the preceding section provided us with three essentially independent measures of the impact of this phase. First, we had the observations which the television production manager had recorded. Second, we could compare the responses with the 48 items which appeared in both the pretest and posttest interviews; such comparisons would indicate attitude shifts as a result of experimental manipulation. We could make these comparisons for both the experimental group and the control group. Finally, we had the participants' own reports reflecting their experience and evaluation of the video-tape recorder.

❧ OBSERVATIONS ❧

Our production manager's observations were of necessity highly subjective. When we consider, however, that they were made by a trained professional observer, carefully recorded during and after each subject's performance, it is easy to recognize their value. To present these reports in detail would not serve much purpose; however, so the reader may get some idea of an individual's reaction to being "forced" to use a technical innovation to which he is basically opposed, we will present summaries for ten of the study's participants.

EXP-ITV "A" He was cooperative during preproduction tape and seems assured that this experiment with video-tape recorder is a good idea. Despite a lengthy conversation, he still resents the administration's attempts to cram ITV down instructors' throats —with no reduction in teaching load for putting lectures on television. He seems to want to be off campus a great deal.

EXP-ITV "B" He brought an almost completed and well-organized lecture outline with him. He made use of films. After finishing preproduction tape, he seemed rather indifferent to the whole process. This apparent change from his original attitude, which was rather enthusiastic, was probably due to the complexity of production. (Seemingly, most of those who go to such elaborate preparations lose interest when the actual taping begins, perhaps because they feel relegated to an inferior position.) His VTR, or video-tape record, is tremendous, with a total of 17 splices, but still, overall, it is a good tape. Generally, he seemed to bring a strong sense of the theatrical into his performance. Yet, most of the operating staff regard this subject's performance as one of the most dynamic.

EXP-ITV "C" He saw no need for a preproduction tape, since he had been on VTR many times before. He reacted favorably to the taping session. He presented a good lecture, and his final tape is good.

EXP-ITV "D" He was ready to make full tape and appeared to be very sociable. He read almost his entire lecture from notes, which showed considerable advance preparation. He displayed much ego involvement with the project. The end result is a good tape with a fair performance.

EXP-ITV "E" His preproduction tape is good; he asked for help freely. His final tape, in which he used some film and charts, is also good. His is a clean and uncluttered presentation. He tried hard and seems convinced that television can be used as a "tool."

EXP-ITV "F" His preproduction tape is good. He was very critical of himself. While watching the "playback," he made careful notes. He got the point of how VTR can be used to improve teaching—probably for the first time. He is not sold on using too many charts and other visual aids. The quality of his final tape is good. He seemed to have learned quite a bit from the experience. He was pleased with how little time it actually took to make the tape.

EXP-ITV "G" During pretape he was fairly hostile. He wanted to get in as much material as possible. He seemed fairly uninterested in the whole thing, but he did give it a good try.

EXP-ITV "H" He was cooperative during pretape. His final tape is good, but he probably made only fair use of television's potential as far as his own course was concerned. He was cooperative and well prepared. He admitted how well he got along without students around. He seemed unconvinced about the possibilities of VTR for improving teaching; however, he wanted to improve his own performance by making a tape again someday.

EXP-ITV "I" He produced a ten-minute preproduction tape. He was worried about his accent and pronunciation. Generally, he produced a good final tape. His content matter was rather complex. He adapted to television very nicely and seemed to evaluate his experience easily.

EXP-ITV "J" His final tape made tremendous use of models for demonstration purposes. He did a good job, was cooperative, had worked hard in preparation, and was easy to direct.

Generalizing on the basis of these admittedly subjective observations, we feel justified to conclude that the elements necessary for "compliance" were present in this experimental phase. Apparently, the professors—once they had decided to "take the bull by the horns"—were willing and able to put their best effort into the ITV project. Despite occasionally uninterested or even hostile behavior, the participants went through with the experiment and, for the most part, produced adequate, if not outstanding, final tapes.

❦ *ATTITUDE CHANGES* ❦

If our study demonstrates that social psychological research in the form of careful observations and rigorous testing of theory can lead to valuable insights into human attitudes and behavior, it also abundantly shows the host of vicissitudes encountered in this type of investigation. Our subjects, the professors, were obviously neither in test tubes nor cages. Before, during, and after the experimental phase, they continued to live in their everyday world with its myriad of influences quite beyond our control. These factors, along with others, made the treatment and interpretation of data in this section particularly difficult.

The theoretical basis of this aspect of our data analysis required a slight regrouping of our control subjects. The reader will recall that our EXP-ITV group of 20 faculty members was bracketed by a control group of 100 instructors. This latter group was now divided into two units.

The first of these subgroups, labeled Control Group I (CONTR. I), was not actively involved in the experimental phase; nevertheless, its members had heard about the video-taping effort. From this group, comprised of 29 subjects, 10 reported they had heard opinions against the VTR experiment; 4 had heard an opinion in favor of it; 4 had heard mixed feelings expressed toward the project; and 13 stated that they had heard something about it, but were vague about the specific attitudes they had heard expressed. This information was obtained at the beginning of the posttest interview.

The second of these control groups, classified as Control Group II (CONTR. II) because they *had not heard* about the experimental phase, was made up of 71 respondents who had been involved in the pretest interview and 68 respondents who had taken part in the posttest interview. This information was obtained during the posttest interview.

Thus, our matrix for comparing responses with the repeat

questions to determine attitude modification can be graphically seen in Figure 3.

In the analysis of the differences in responses obtained at the original interview and the re-interview, placement of an absolute value on tests of significance was impossible for two critical reasons:

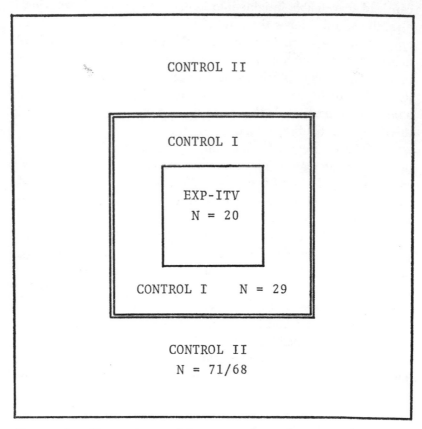

FIGURE 3. Categories used for comparison of pretest with posttest differences. The two groups within double line either participated in or had some knowledge of the experimental phase.

The groups of subjects who had some knowledge of the video-tape experiment consisted of a combined total of 49 subjects, indicating that we were dealing with a relatively small sample. In the determination of significance levels, sample size and absolute differences correlate negatively. Therefore, very high differences would have been required to yield statistically significant results. More important, in order to carry out the content analysis which provided us with the highly revealing attitudes of the faculty for and against ITV, extremely discrete response categories had to be created. Thus, we found ourselves with a relatively small number of responses in each of a large number of response categories.

Consequently, in the data presented in this section, tests of significance which yielded levels of confidence even approaching .10 are reported, but, of course, these should not be interpreted as indicating anything more than slight trends.

However, for the EXP-ITV group of subjects, we undertook a careful person-by-person qualitative analysis of attitude change. These data, which we will present at the end of this chapter, will not only include the pretest and posttest differences but also an analysis of the personal reports from both the subjects and the television production coordinator.

In the EXP-ITV data, five items yielded differences between the responses to those questions which approached significance at the .10 level of confidence. Two of these shifts suggested modification in a direction more favorable to ITV. One of these shifts was expressed by an increased "willingness to accept ITV as a replacement for classroom lectures"; the other was reflected by the absence in the posttest of the response "I don't know, but I am against ITV," which had occurred three times in the pretest.

Remarks expressing the thought that ITV would "limit the number of qualified instructors," which indicated a shift in a less favorable direction, appeared once in the pretest and five times in the posttest interview. Also on the anti-ITV side of the ledger, the number of miscellaneous responses against ITV increased from the pretest to the posttest. The response suggesting that ITV would "ease teaching load and give more time for research" reflected an-

113

other attitude shift by appearing seven times in the pretest and only twice in the posttest.

Two items appeared in the CONTR. I group which—at the .10 level of confidence—approached significance. As was the case with the EXP-ITV group, a favorable shift occurred in the item related to accepting ITV as a replacement for classroom lectures. The other item, which was extremely difficult to interpret within the pro-ITV and anti-ITV framework, concerned the relationship of television instruction to "size of class." Five respondents on the pretest viewed large classes as more suitable for ITV than small classes, as compared with one respondent in the posttest.

Oddly enough, we found, statistically, the highest significant difference involving pretest and posttest responses among the CONTR. II group. Chi squares for six response categories were significant at a level of confidence of .05 or better. We think that these apparent attitude changes may be spurious, a contention for which we will present some basis in the next section. Nevertheless, to complete the statistical analysis, here are the items which showed such modification and its extent. Two items indicated a change in a favorable direction, significant at the .01 level. These were "ITV gives bad results" (pretest, 7; posttest, 0) and "ITV impersonal and mass production" (pretest, 3; posttest, 0). Similarly, two categories of items reflected changes significant at the .05 level of confidence. These were miscellaneous responses of "Favor ITV" (pretest, 19; posttest, 31) and the overall ratings on the favorable-unfavorable-neutral scale of responses to four different ITV items (pretest, 33-34-4; posttest, 31-24-13). This group showed only one unfavorable shift, which was on the item "ITV does not motivate students" (pretest, 4; posttest, 11), significant at the .05 level of confidence.

We need to reiterate that the small number of subjects in the two critical groups—the EXP-ITV group and the CONTR. II subgroup—coupled with the small number of responses found in many of the categories, greatly reduced the possibility of a definitive analysis of the data. Any attempt to read into these findings anything more than an indication, in very broad terms, of direction of attitude shifts for or against ITV would be unjustifiable. Even when we now make a somewhat grosser comparison of pretest and posttest results, the above caution must remain in effect.

The discrete responses to the 48 items were now collapsed into three categories, which we established by employing the same raing technique we had used in the original content analysis. With the aid of this classification of ITV attitudes as favorable, no opinion, or against, we were able to construct a 2 x 3 chi square table of all responses to the same question on the pretest and posttest interviews.[1] It also permitted a broader examination of the shifts which had occurred in each of the three categories for each of our three groups. We shall present this overview first. Because there was an overall reduction in the responses in all cases, ranging from 5 per cent in the EXP-ITV group to 24 per cent and 25 per cent in the CONTR. I and CONTR. II groups respectively, a comparison of the actual frequencies in each of the response categories would be misleading. Instead, we present in Table 7 the per cent of total responses falling into each category for the pretest and posttest interviews for each of our groups. We provide further breakdown of the EXP-ITV data by separately giving the percentages of total responses for Departments "A" and "B."

As will be apparent, the changes in percentages shown in the table may not be as statistically significant as they might have been if a larger group of subjects had been involved. Nevertheless, the table does indicate trends in attitude changes which are in the predicted direction. Thus, the overall EXP-ITV shows an increase of 7.7 per cent in the favorable responses with a corresponding decrease of 6.6 per cent in the unfavorable column. Department "A" shows the highest apparent attitude shift, with an increase of 13.5 per cent on the favorable and a 12.5 per cent decrease on the unfavorable side. Less change apparently occurred in the Department

[1] We are indebted to the late Carl Hovland for suggesting this type of analysis.

TABLE 7

PERCENTAGE OF TOTAL PRETEST AND POSTTEST RESPONSES
CATEGORIZED AS FAVORABLE, UNFAVORABLE, AND NEUTRAL

Group	Total Responses (100%)	Per cent Favorable	Per cent Neutral	Per cent Unfavorable
EXP-ITV				
Pretest	(238)	48.3	5.5	46.2
Posttest	(227)	56.0	4.4	39.6
Dept. "A"				
Pretest	(107)	44.9	3.7	51.4
Posttest	(113)	58.4	2.7	38.9
Dept. "B"				
Pretest	(132)	49.2	6.8	43.9
Posttest	(114)	53.5	6.1	40.4
CONTR I (Had heard)				
Pretest	(357)	48.5	3.0	48.5
Posttest	(272)	53.6	4.4	43.0
CONTR II (Had not heard)				
Pretest	(697)	49.4	3.3	47.3
Posttest	(527)	50.3	5.7	44.0

"B" group, with only a 4.3 per cent shift toward a more favorable position and a 3.59 per cent shift away from an unfavorable position. Similar changes were recorded for Control Group I, showing 5.1 per cent more favorable responses and 5.5 per cent fewer unfavorable responses. Clearly, the least change occurred in the Control Group II, which shows only a .9 per cent increase in the favorable responses and a 3.3 per cent decrease in the unfavorable column, most of which apparently shifted to the neutral categories, increasing them by 2.4 per cent. A graphic comparison indicating per cent of change in the number of favorable and unfavorable responses for each of the three main groups is shown in Figure 4.

Along with the results of the chi squares computed for the differences in the responses between pretest and posttest interviews

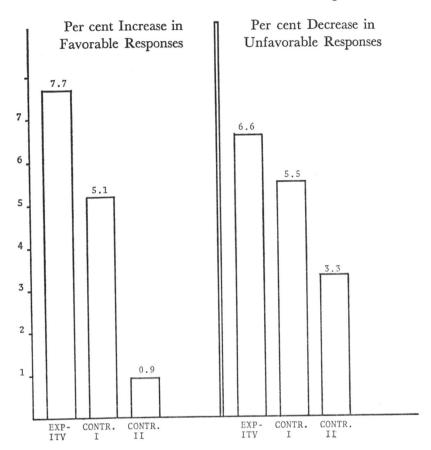

FIGURE 4. Percentage increase in favorable responses and percentage decrease in unfavorable responses from pretest interview to posttest interview for groups of subjects.

(see Table 8), we are including as a point of interest those items which were most representative in attitude shifts.

For the EXP-ITV group, the difference between the pretest and posttest distribution of responses yielded a chi square value significant at only the .26 level of confidence. But it does suggest a change in the hypothesized direction, with the "favor" responses

TABLE 8

CHI SQUARES COMPUTED BETWEEN PRETEST AND POSTTEST
TOTAL NUMBER OF RESPONSES TO 48 IDENTICAL ITEMS

Group Category	Number Subjects	Chi Square	p
Experimental	20	2.77	0.26
Department "A"	9	4.28	0.12
Department "B"	11	0.44	0.95
Control I	29	2.16	0.35
Control II			
Pretest	71	1.50	0.60*
Posttest	68		

* See text.

increasing and the "against" responses decreasing. In this group, the mean number of responses per item for the 48 repeat questions was 10. After viewing the data from several vantage points, we arbitrarily decided to examine all response categories which reflected an increase or decrease of 5 or more responses. A shift in the favorable direction we defined as a reduction of "against" responses and/or an increase of "favorable" responses. There were 12 such categories for the EXP-ITV's, 8 of which shifted in a favorable direction. These categories and the number of response shifts were as follows: "Lack of personal contact" (14); "Extent to which ITV could replace conventional classroom instruction" (12); "ITV instruction doesn't motivate students" (6); opinions opposed to ITV instruction not classifiable into other response categories (6); "Interaction left out" (6); "Outstanding lecturers available" (5); "More difficult to teach on TV" (5); and "Number of qualified ITV instructors is limited" (5).

Responses which shifted in the "against" direction were the following: unclassifiable pro-ITV responses (10); "ITV useful as a supplement" (6); and "ITV eases teacher's load" (5).

When we again divided the experimental group by departments, the chi squares computed on the differences in the pretest and posttest distributions of favorable, neutral, and "against" responses were significant at the following levels: differences in the responses of Department "A," .12, and of Department "B," .95. Department "B" decreased in responding from the pretest to the posttest in all three categories, while respondents from Department "A" increased in favorable responses and decreased in unfavorable responses.

Differences in the pretest and posttest responses of the CONTR. II group yielded a chi square significant at the .35 level. The mean number of responses for each of the 48 items was 13. Again after viewing the data, we derived an arbitrary basis for analysis. In this instance, we decided to examine any specific item which resulted in a shift of responses of 7 or more items in the same direction. Of the 5 that evidenced such shifts, the following 3— again shown with their respective frequency of change—were in a favorable direction: "Imagine yourself against ITV" appeared in a miscellaneous group of responses (15); "Eases teacher's load" (7); and "Lack of personal contact" (18). Items for this group which shifted in an unfavorable direction were as follows: "ITV instruction reaches more students" (5); and "ITV useful as a supplement" (11).

In CONTR. II the computation of the chi squares for the pretest-versus-posttest distribution of favor, no opinion, and against responses revealed that neutral responses in this group accrued in an approximately equal number for those favorable to ITV and against it in the pretest. Including these neutral responses might introduce a spurious indication of attitude shift. With the neutral response categories eliminated, the differences were significant at the .60 level of confidence.

The mean number of responses per item for the CONTR. II group was 25. Again, based on the characteristics of the data, an arbitrary decision was made. We examined those items which showed a shift of 13 or more responses in the same direction. This criterion was met by 2 items shifting in one direction and 2 shifting in the other. Among the against-ITV responses, "Lack of personal contact" appeared 57 times in the pretest responses but only 14

119

times in the posttest responses. Miscellaneous reasons that the respondent gave when he "imagined self against ITV" decreased from 34 responses on the pretest to 12 on the posttest. The 2 items which showed a shift in the *against* direction were as follows: "Favor ITV" because it "Reaches more students" (pretest, 43; posttest, 11); and "ITV useful as a supplement" (pretest, 27; posttest, 6). Although no statistically significant differences were revealed, we could thus identify at least a trend in attitude change in the predicted direction. In other words, when compared with those who neither participated nor communicated with participants in the ITV project, those who did participate or did talk to participants appeared to become at least somewhat more favorably disposed to ITV.

❧ THE EXPERIMENTAL GROUP ❧

As indicated in the preceding section, the small size of the experimental group, combined with the nature of the chi square test of significance, clearly suggested that the mere lack of statistical significance between the pretest and the posttest—admittedly in the predicted direction—did not preclude the possibility that critical attitude shifts had occurred. In natural behavioral-setting research such as we incorporated in our investigation, an "eye ball," as well as statistical, analysis of the results appeared to be worthwhile.

First of all, the results of the posttest interview were compared with the reports of both the television production coordinator and those written by the participants themselves. Comparisons of responses, when collapsed to the overall three-point scale used earlier—favorable, neutral, or unfavorable—indicated that the reports correlated to a surprisingly high degree with the responses from the posttest interview.

Table 9 shows that although the attitudes of a total of nine professors were apparently unaffected by the experimental situation, a total of nine others actually shifted to an attitude more favorable toward ITV than the pretest responses indicated, while two more shifted in a less favorable direction.

Of the unchanged group, four were originally favorable to ITV; four were unfavorable; and one was neutral. Thus, these data do reflect patterns consistent with the theoretical formulations on

TABLE 9

FREQUENCY, DIRECTION, AND NATURE OF ATTITUDE SHIFTS
OF PROFESSORS INVOLVED IN VTR PHASE OF INVESTIGATION

Direction	Departments and Frequencies		Total Frequencies
	"A"	"B"	
Favorable			
Unfavorable to favorable	1	1	2
Neutral to favorable	3	1	4
Unfavorable to neutral	1	2	3
Total	5	4	9
Unfavorable			
Favorable to unfavorable	0	0	0
Neutral to unfavorable	0	2	2
Favorable to neutral	0	0	0
Total	0	2	2
Unchanged			
Favor	2	2	4
Neutral	0	1	1
Unfavorable	2	2	4
Total	4	5	9

attitude change involving the effects of a forced-compliance situation. We could hypothesize that, to some extreme groups or groups with dogmatic attitudes, dissonance may be introduced into existing cognitive structures with the least effect on their basic nature. In the present investigation, this fact was reflected by either "no change" in attitude or by a shift to a neutral feeling. But only in two instances in the entire sample did we observe an extreme shift from an against position to a favorable one.

We might also hypothesize that if a situation—resulting from conditions similar to those in our experiment—proves to be compatible to subjects who already favor ITV, this attitude would shift in an even more favorable direction. Although this was not recorded by our relatively crude three-point scale, impressionistic evidence indicated that in two instances involving the apparently "unchanged" group, a shift to an even more favorable attitude did occur.

According to theoretical expectations, the "neutral" group should have recorded the greatest instance of attitude change. Six of the nine subjects who reflected an attitude shift were, indeed, scaled as neutral in responses on the pretest interview. Of course, in the neutral group, two subjects shifted in an unfavorable direction as well. In a way, no one should regard this as an unexpected reaction when he considers the potentially ego-threatening and ego-involving atmosphere in which, for the first time, a professor must contemplate his own image projected from a television tape. In fact, that this potentially negative effect of the experimental procedure occurred in only two instances is surprising.

Perhaps the most significant result of the present investigation—in behavioral rather than in cognitive terms—is that, of the two departments involved, one subsequently began offering a telecourse, a move which it had previously rejected, and that the other began using some of its own video-taped material as a supplement to its traditional teaching efforts.

We are acutely aware that, along with the many ongoing institutional influences on these departments, it would be misleading to suggest that in this instance "correlation necessarily meant causation," particularly since the data from our control group were, in the strictest sense, inconclusive. However, informal discussions with some members of these two departments suggest that, all things considered, the experimental situation did play a role in departmental decision making with respect to the use of ITV. However, lacking systematically derived data on the actual decision-making processes in these two departments, we cannot adequately determine the extent of the effect that participation, overt or covert, had in our experimental situation. Our pretest and posttest data, like all attitude measures, give us merely inferential data concerning the probability of actual behavior. As indicated earlier, Metro University has since curtailed—at least temporarily—all telecourses. So, at best, a short-term rather than a long-range effect was all that was possible to achieve even if our experiment did have a maximum effect on the participating departments.

EIGHT

VIEWS
FROM
NINE
UNIVERSITIES

Inevitably, the data we have presented raise the question of their value for generalization. Are the findings of our study generally applicable to other populations of college professors and other innovations than ITV? Or are these findings merely artifacts of the particular sample which we chose to exam-

ine? We are fully aware that a definitive answer to this question requires a duplication of our investigation at other universities. However, we also believed some value would come from submitting our findings to a more subjective test, that is, presenting them to members of other academic communities and asking them to respond to them in a relatively informal interview setting. The findings that we report in this chapter, then, are not the result of the same systematic investigation we used in our research case history. Nevertheless, they may give some indication of whether the results of our research case history are at least fairly universal or whether they are primarily related to ITV as we observed it at Metro University. On this basis, we gathered further data from nine additional colleges and universities, some being comparable with Metro and others being distinctly different. As indicated earlier, they varied in size, source of sponsorship and support, and geographical location.[1]

[1] Specifically, the universities and colleges we visited were Hofstra University, Michigan State University, San Francisco State College, Southern Methodist University, State

124

❦ *PROCEDURES AND INTERVIEW FORMAT* ❦

The procedure for this phase of our investigation was as follows. We contacted a prominent faculty member at each of these nine institutions and asked him to serve as a local consultant for our project and to arrange individual appointments with three or more of the institution's key administrators. These included, among others, presidents, vice presidents, and deans of faculties, arts and sciences, and graduate schools. Where appropriate, appointments were also made with the top administrators directly concerned with television instruction and audio-visual programs. Thus, the individuals in our project represent a sampling of approximately 27 administrators who were quite directly involved with important decision making and the diffusion of innovations on their respective campuses.

A second group which each of our local consultants was asked to call together was a heterogeneous faculty group representing as many academic areas as possible, including the humanities, social sciences, physical sciences, education, and the more technical fields such as engineering and architecture. We assured both the administrators and the faculty participants that neither their individual names nor the names of institutions would be used in reporting specific findings. We felt that granting such anonymity, in addition to obvious ethical considerations, would contribute to a freer expression of opinions and feelings.

After making these arrangements, we then set up schedules for visits to the campuses. Typically, the interviews with individual administrators were limited to 20 to 30 minutes each. Meetings with the faculty groups generally consisted of one- to two-hour sessions, frequently around the luncheon table. Wherever possible, all participants—the administrators and faculty members—were given the opportunity to read the preliminary report of the research case his-

University of Buffalo, Texas Christian University, Trinity University, University of Pittsburgh, and Washington University.

tory. However, to assure that everyone had some background information, the interviewer briefly presented the highlights of the Metro University study and then posed a number of open-end questions. Although these questions necessarily varied somewhat in format—depending on the particular institution, the respondents, and the setting—they essentially involved the following content:

1. If an innovation was to be started on your campus, how would you go about instituting it, or how do you think others would institute it?
2. Give some concrete examples of innovations that have been attempted on your campus, and trace the effect of these innovations.
3. How do you (or did you, or would you) react to the success or failure of utilizing instructional television on your campus?
4. What is your reaction to our description of the prototype for the cosmopolite instructor who is broadly accepting of innovation as opposed to the laggard or localite who broadly rejects innovation? To what degree are types which would fit these attitude patterns present on your campus? If they are present, are there academic areas where they can be found in greater or lesser concentration? Where do you think resistance to innovation is most likely to take place?
5. Can you give a general picture of the decision-making process with respect to innovation on your campus?

Obviously, these questions were general enough to stimulate as much discussion as possible. Informality was emphasized particularly in the meetings with faculty groups, and the questions were presented in such a manner as to avoid undue defensiveness. The questions—as may be apparent—had been designed not only to provide information on the degree that we might generalize our more narrowly focused ITV findings but also to probe carefully into some of the other areas which we thought might be related to the broader field of innovation in higher education—for example, areas concerning the personality make-up of the professor that might relate to the results of our factor analysis. In a sense, then, we feel that while these interviews give some indication about how much we can generalize our research findings at Metro, they may be even more helpful in developing further hypotheses about the broader issues—to be tested in future research.

❧ ANALYSIS OF RESPONSES ❧

In almost every interview or discussion, one of the first challenges that the interviewer had to meet was that of defining the concept of innovation. Of course, the interviewees had their own definitions for the term; often the interviewer—and, in many cases, the interviewee—became quite aware that individuals differ sharply on what to include under the heading of innovation. We had come to accept the term as relating to an object or idea which represents a major change in the methods employed to achieve the basic goals of a given institution. For our purposes it was irrelevant whether an innovation was new in the absolute sense or simply new to a particular school. For example, we accepted the recent introduction of a language laboratory on one campus as an innovation, even though many schools had adopted such a program years ago. The question of what constitutes a major change is even more difficult to answer. As we will see, what appears to be a minor change in, let us say, one university's curriculum may loom as a major revolution in another; to still another it may represent a minor readjustment to be handled by a memorandum from the academic dean's office.

But, in actuality, the issue went much further than the above would indicate. Most of our respondents felt that generalizations concerning innovations were difficult, if not impossible. Frequently, they suggested that the use of more restrictive modifiers might make some generalizations possible, but often this approach led to very narrow definitions of questionable usefulness. Classifications of innovations included those based on the nature of the innovation itself—for example, technical versus non-technical change —or those involving subjective change rather than changes in

127

methodology. Other classifications were based on the number of institutional substructures potentially involved. Thus, respondents viewed changes within a department quite differently from those which involved entire divisions, such as the college of arts and sciences and the engineering school. Closely related to these classifications were those categories which were based on the original source of the innovation. Some respondents pointed out that changes proposed by the university board and instituted by the president frequently meet with a different response from those instituted by a department chairman. Of course, the categories under discussion are not necessarily mutually exclusive. Some interviewees felt that the response to a technical innovation introduced by the administration on a university-wide basis would be quite different from the response to the same innovation introduced at the departmental level. This led the authors to conclude that the term "innovation" without modification may be of limited value, particularly in programmed research where precise definition is imperative.

Among the specific changes which administrators and faculty members described to us we found—perhaps not surprisingly —very few technical innovations. Most of the ones they reported involved changes in curriculum or course content with a minimum of alteration in teaching method. Most frequently mentioned were the launching of an honors program, and coordination of the core curricula—for example, instituting a required humanities course during the first and second year in the liberal-arts college. Innovations designed to improve the relationship between students and the university also received frequent mention. Spurred on, no doubt, by student unrest in many parts of the country, administrators and faculty members were attempting to find ways to provide students with more participation in school affairs or, at least, to provide more adequate channels of communication for reducing the ever more visible psychological distance between students and faculty. However, these attempts were generally quite timid, and emphasis was repeatedly placed on their highly experimental nature. The limited range of such changes can be illustrated by the comments made at one school which had just developed a faculty-student senate. While more student participation in some school affairs is desirable, some administrators and faculty members asserted, students should not have a voice in developing course curricula because they are on campus only a short time and are in no way qualified to make decisions at this level.

We do not wish to deny the very real impact that the changes or innovations we have mentioned above can have on a particular institution. A change from a liberal-arts core curriculum of several individual courses taught by members of separate departments to a two-year humanities course coordinated by an interdisciplinary program can constitute a significant innovation, with all the characteristics we have attributed to this form of change. But we suspect that highly superficial changes occur which have little or no effect on the major processes of a university. Often these changes are not even new to the particular institution. Seemingly, a teaching system goes along for some time, then suddenly some pressure arises for a change. It can be a minor curriculum change or a major one such as a shift from Mortimer Adler's Neo-Scholasticist focus on a Great Books program to a system of a more traditional curriculum. Is the latter in fact historically an innovation? Actually, since traditional teaching methods existed before the Great Books program and since traditional teaching is to a large extent built on neo-scholastic concepts, neither of these ideas is really new in a historical sense. Many, if not most, schools appear to play a similar kind of game of musical chairs with innovations, where one "innovation" replaces still another and so on. Universities act as if the number of such changes is fixed, so that eventually the system returns to a method which has been tried before and which has either been abandoned or has become, in a sense, covertly institutionalized—that is, institutionalized but held in abeyance for later reactivation.

We have found that one of the areas most frequently involved in this circle of changes relates to the best use of the faculty's time. Let us assume an institution at a certain stage feels

129

that the professor can make the best use of his time by lecturing only twice a week to large classes of undergraduate students and then devoting himself to consultations in a tutorial sense with individual undergraduate and graduate students. After a while, the pattern is changed slightly. The professor's lecture sections are now supplemented by discussion periods led by graduate students. Later, when the school decides that graduate students are inadequate in their instruction, the large lecture sections are eliminated and the individual professor is asked to teach a large number of smaller classes. When the school finally sees this as an uneconomical use of his time, it reverts again to using large lecture sections. Interestingly enough, almost every institution included in our sample reported innovations to us which could be placed at some point in such cycles.

A similar pattern develops in connection with changes in teaching methods. Many schools have continuous or periodic teacher evaluation and committees charged with the responsibility for improving teaching. The innovations reported in this area are even more sparse than in those areas we have discussed. Usually, these committees have extremely obscure and diffuse criteria, and, within the safe confines of their own membership, they vaguely discuss ideas for getting the professor to pay more attention to his students, to spend more time on preparing his lectures, to involve himself in more or, perhaps, less research, or to participate more actively in the total life of the academic community. As one of our interviewees pointed out, "Our evaluation committee is for the most part a mutual admiration society." Another respondent said, "Our improvement-of-teaching committee is dedicated to the perpetuation of criteria-free evaluations." A university in our sample reported some success in evaluating teaching methods by opening these committee sessions to invited students and members of the board and community supporters of the school. This program was too new to judge as to its impact on the changing of teaching methods, but the faculty's response to such an innovation was far from unanimously favorable.

130

❦ *SOURCES OF INNOVATIONS* ❦

The sources of innovations in higher education are as diverse as the innovations themselves. We found that almost every segment within the academic community can initiate change, including students and individual faculty members. In addition to these, several sources of innovations exist outside the university. We feel a number of interesting issues need to be explored in relation to these sources. As we have mentioned earlier, research in the diffusion of new agricultural methods and new pharmaceutical products emphasizes the important role of the "change agent"; in the first instance, he is a county agent and in the second, he is a drug-detail man. Such change agents are virtually non-existent in higher education. Book salesmen who contact faculty members cannot be considered change agents in this sense, since they are merely promoting more of the same products. (Parenthetically, we might mention that an increasing number of textbook publishers have become interested in producing educational films, tapes, slides, or programmed techniques as supplements to or replacements for traditional textbooks. However, as one editor pointed out, salesmen will first have to be trained to sell professors on the idea of using new instructional media in general before they can sell them specific materials or equipment.) Some faculty members seem to be aware that little outside effort is being made to persuade them to adopt new teaching methods and techniques. In spite of many government and foundation programs, several of our respondents readily admitted their own ignorance about such things as video-tape recorders, teaching machines, computer-assisted systems, and other technical innovations; furthermore, they seemed unaware as to where they could learn about them. Particularly interesting was the frequent ignorance expressed concerning the services of audio-visual departments on their own campuses.

Innovations do seem to follow certain predictable routes—predictable, that is, for a particular institution. Perhaps these patterns are closely related to the more basic nature of the institutional structure. If the administration characteristically avoids "shoving changes down its professors' throats," most innovations originate at the faculty or departmental level. Seemingly, once such a pattern has become established, changes initiated at the top tend to be opposed by the rank-and-file faculty member regardless of their merits. Conversely, the highly hierarchically structured institution generates innovations at the board and administration level and filters them down through the department chairmen to the faculty. In a few schools, the power seems to rest with the department chairman, particularly where such chairmanships are permanent appointments and may change less often than the top administration. In several cases in our sample, the administrative and the faculty segment both felt that the other was responsible for initiating innovation; as a result, the rather humorous picture presents itself of two people listening on the same telephone line with neither of them saying anything.

Even where sources exist for generating ideas about new approaches in higher education, economic factors tend to present a serious barrier to their adoption. Most university budgets are fixed from year to year, and—though careful analysis is necessary here— some evidence shows that these budgets tend to support the existing system. Allocation systems seem to provide little or nothing in the way of built-in mechanisms for change. We were often told, of course, that many innovations in higher education can be accomplished within existing budgets, but drastic changes requiring rechanneling of funds often take years to clear the budget hurdle, if they clear it at all. Basically, we would hypothesize that the economics of the university system and the entire budgeting procedures too often appear to be dedicated to maintaining the status quo.

A few financial sources outside the university are sometimes available for introducing a specific innovation on a campus. Various agencies, public and private, have made such funds available, particularly among those institutions ranking in the lower part of the academic scale which are frequently attended by socially and culturally deprived students. However, we believe that such guaranteed financing in no way assures the institutionalizing of a new idea. If channels within the system for the diffusion of innovations are non-existent, a very high probability exists that they will become accepted only at a very superficial level.

One other source of innovation deserves mention here, and that is private industry in the local community. This source of new ideas and their economic implementation is far from widespread, but we found it to be an important factor in at least two institutions. Often it involves only a very narrow academic field, usually in the more technical areas like engineering or business administration. Innovations here included two-way television hookups between a large manufacturing plant and a university lecture room, providing corporation personnel as visiting lecturers in the university's classroom. Obviously such innovations serve a number of purposes. Most important among these may be the exchange between the university and industry which itself may give rise to new innovations simply because it forces members of the academic community to relate to those outside the system.

❧ DIFFUSION, INSTITUTIONALIZATION, AND REVERSION ❧

Our discussions on the nine campuses clearly indicate the need for intensive empirical study to determine the fate of an innovation in higher education over a long period of time. Our interviews make it abundantly clear that overt acceptance and what we will call institutionalization of the innovation are two quite different stages with a number of intermediate steps. We would postulate two major patterns of development. Both would begin with an overt acceptance of a new idea or method, for example, they would begin with the operation of an ITV program; but while in one pattern this will lead to institutionalization, in the other a kind of "pseudo acceptance" occurs. Although the program in the latter

133

instance may continue over a considerable period of time, it never really becomes part of the institution, and at a given point a convenient excuse is found to terminate it. Under these circumstances, the chances for its being re-established appear to be very slim indeed, even though the hardware, the cameras, the receivers, and other equipment are still available and are even sometimes readapted for other uses, such as adult education or public relations. In the other pattern, where institutionalization has taken place, such acceptance may actually be quite covert, and although the program may be discarded at some later date, the innovation is added to the pool of educational methods with a fairly high probability that it will eventually be revived.

This hypothesis leads us to advocate great caution in drawing conclusions simply on the basis of overt presence or absence of an innovation. Basic research is needed to hunt for factors which indicate covert acceptance. One key to this search might be the conditions under which the innovation was rejected. If the original overt acceptance led to an experience which most or all of the members of the system viewed as basically negative, then chances for institutionalization are unlikely; as a result, we would predict that the probability is very low that the innovation, once abandoned, will be reinstated. On the other hand, if the termination of a new program is brought about by economic factors or by a limited but effective opposition—for example, simply because one powerful administrator is opposed to it—some covert institutionalization may have taken place, with at least some possibility of a reinstatement of the innovation if the circumstances change. These are purely conjectures on our part, but we feel that they suggest important hypotheses which bear further investigation.

In part, the high mortality rate of innovations in higher education may be a function of the original acceptance in yet another way. From our interviews we have learned that administrators and faculty members alike find it difficult, if not impossible, to evaluate the merits and demerits of a new idea prior to or even after its adoption. Hence, most, if not all, innovations are adopted on an experimental basis; the tentativeness of such acceptance our respondents frequently pointed out to us. When an administrator states that "We have set up a faculty-student senate on a trial basis for one year and if it doesn't work, we can always disband it, just as we earlier disbanded the faculty-student forum," we believe the built-in mechanism for abandoning such an innovation would almost certainly prevent any degree of institutionalization. In other words, it is not just the experimental nature of the original adoption but often the authority inherent in a group to terminate innovation that prevents total acceptance. Once an innovation has been terminated, a system clearly has only two choices: It can move on to another innovation—and, indeed, some systems move from one innovation to another—or it can revert to old tried-and-true methods. The latter appears to be more often the choice, but this area is another in which we feel further research is needed.

❧ CONFIRMATION OF FINDINGS ❧

Because one major purpose of these interviews was to obtain responses from a broad sample of professors and administrators to our specific ITV findings in our research case history, we allocated a considerable amount of time at each meeting to elicit attitudes toward instructional television. The overall picture emerging from these interviews is amazingly clear-cut on this point: Most, if not all, of our findings are confirmed. Admittedly, our sample was too small to permit a truly scientific generalization. Nine institutions, 27 administrators, and some 75 faculty members do not constitute an adequate sample of higher education in the United States. Furthermore, we did not meet with faculty members individually but, rather, in groups, which may have had a decisive influence on their responses. Nevertheless, we feel that these groups and individual administrators represented enough of a heterogeneous sample to lead us to postulate that the findings of our case study are not restricted to one institution, although some question may exist as to whether they are restricted in part to one type—or at least a particular type—of innovation.

The first thing that clearly emerges from our discussions on other campuses is that attitudes toward ITV appear to transcend the structural, as well as other, characteristics of the institution itself. Seemingly, attitudes toward ITV are more generic to the teaching role as perceived by the faculty member, although our sample was too small and our interviewing techniques too inadequate to do more than hypothesize in this area. But we were impressed with the apparent consistency of attitudes toward ITV, regardless of an institution's size, its urban or rural location, its sponsorship, or even its past experience or inexperience with television as an instructional device.

An overwhelming majority of our interviewees on these campuses were hostile to ITV. Perhaps the most amazing aspect of their negative attitude was the similarity of the reasons they gave for resisting instructional television. Without exception—wherever reasons for resisting ITV were elaborated—we found patterns of responses similar and sometimes identical to those reported in our research case history. Some of our interviewees gave sound, rational, and objective reasons, but, at the same time, others gave a myriad of irrational and emotional responses with which we were now familiar. These responses implied that ITV represents some sort of a threat to their very existence or that it is a kind of toy which has no place in any educational institution of serious academic orientation.

The provocative responses we received from two professors on different campuses offered one of the most interesting examples of the kind of reasoning in which sophisticated teachers can engage —and certainly a further caution against making value judgments in psychological research in innovation at universities. One professor who was a distinguished behavioral scientist with a record of unusual interest in innovation in his own field would be described as a cosmopolite by any standard. With respect to the use of ITV

136

at universities, he stated that experimental adoption of television instruction may comprise a genuine trial period. Professors really seriously consider its use during this period but reject it on a sound basis—that is, it really does not do the job of teaching in the most sophisticated sense of the term. A professor at another institution, a very productive biological scientist, also demonstrated an unusual interest in innovation in his own field and was a person who could also be described as a cosmopolite. When the point was made in our interview that universities almost from their inception have maintained essentially the same pattern of instruction, he stated that this persistence of traditional methods actually indicates their superiority.

Here are two respondents, then, who take the stand that the slowness of the university to adopt innovations is no particular indictment of its rigidity as an institution or of the short-sightedness of its professors but, rather, is support for the basis effectiveness of the traditional methods that persist in the institution.

Apparently, the type of television facilities employed in a given program had little effect on faculty attitudes. The question related to this aspect of ITV was of particular interest to us, since Metro University had an open-circuit channel, that is, one that can be received through any television set in the community. In fact, some thought that the chance for public scrutiny might have contributed to the resistance among the Metro faculty. Seemingly, this is not a major contributor to the negative attitude. The nine institutions in our sample in this phase of our investigation had had a wide range of experience with ITV. A few had even used open-circuit television and then switched to closed-circuit television. Some evidence showed that public viewing might appear to be undesirable in a few academic areas where potentially controversial material might be presented, such as in the teaching of history, political science, or even biology, where discussion of evolution might bring criticism in some parts of the country. However, the resistance to ITV was not really predicated primarily upon fear that the general public would view the presentation. A much greater

137

fear appeared to be that instructional television, either open- or closed-circuit, makes the presentation available to the scrutiny of one's colleagues within the university.

Thus, the possible judgment of fellow faculty members seems to be a more likely source of resistance than the possibility of public reaction to controversial material. We are reminded of the almost universal but unwritten ethic that in the university in general (except in medical and dental schools and, perhaps, in some other professional institutions) professors ordinarily do not enter one another's classroom. Why should this be, aside from the belief that such a ban is an extension of academic freedom? Perhaps, many professors have traditionally disliked exposing their teaching methods to the scrutiny of their peers. If professors hold this attitude as universally as we suspect, it is easy to understand why strong resistance to any public viewing of class proceedings will occur. The fact that such viewing might be effected covertly would only increase many professors' anxiety.

Having now postulated that neither the characteristics of the institution nor the type of television equipment appear to have a major bearing on faculty ITV attitudes, we next explored the question of whether, perhaps, certain academic areas are more adaptable than others to teaching on television. Here we found no common agreement among our interviewees, even within one institution. The only generalization we can make is that most agreed that while ITV might have some value in other academic areas, in their own field it was virtually without merit. By way of example, we can report the conversation between a music professor and a math professor during one of our luncheon meetings. The music professor began by pointing out that in his field, television was of absolutely no use since he must completely depend on getting feedback from the student. "I must be sure," he said, "that the student understands one step before moving on to the next." However, he thought that in an area like math, which consists purely of information dissemination and the presentation of formulas that the student must memorize, ITV could be most helpful. Not so, replied the math professor. In teaching mathematics, the teacher must be sure that the student understands the earlier steps leading to a new mathematical formulation. Only by receiving feedback from the student can he be sure that his class is ready for the next step. "However," he added, "I think that a course in music, such as music appreciation, might be taught quite efficiently on television." Conversations like these were typical of those that took place on most of the campuses we visited.

A topic somewhat related to the above debates concerned student attitudes toward ITV courses and their performance in them. We were told by instructors experienced in ITV that students generally resist enrolling in television courses, a confirmation of the findings reported earlier. On student performance we seemed to get two diametrically opposed responses. On those campuses where careful analysis of grades had been undertaken, we were told that no significant differences were apparent in the performance of students taught by television and those who were not. However, where no such empirical data were available, our respondents stated that students perform less well in television courses. The reasons for such poor performance, they often pointed out, were related to the "qualitative differences" of the two methods and the increase in the psychological distance between professor and student resulting from depersonalized television instruction.

One of our most unequivocal findings on these nine campuses relates to the pattern which characterizes the history of instructional television as an innovation. That this pattern transcends all differences between institutions appears almost certain to us. Not only do our interviews confirm this, but at a recent conference[2] experts directly involved in the various phases of the educational television movement and other educators described essentially the same pattern. To be sure, minor variations occur, but the following description appears to be typical.

[2] Meeting of the Media Standards Committee of the Southern Region Education Board relating to an interinstitutional television project. The senior author is a member of the committee.

139

The pattern begins with some source of "seed" money, a private foundation, the federal government, or, in some cases, a source within the university itself. Concurrently, some enthusiastic individual is an advocate of the innovation. He may be a member of the faculty, an administrator, a department head, or possibly an influential board member. Because of his enthusiasm and the availability of funds, the program will be started "on an experimental basis." After installation of equipment, the first one or two courses are telecast and, for quite some time, they may continue to be. In some cases the program is terminated after one showing of the complete course; in another instance it is continued for some years. Generally, however, the program is discontinued for one reason or another. The reversion phenomenon appears despite the original enthusiasm for the program, and the institution returns to the old teaching methods used prior to the introduction of ITV. This is a clear case of what we described earlier as incomplete institutionalization. ITV has never become part of the educational output of the institution, although it seemed at first to have been genuinely accepted. In some cases total abandonment of ITV is avoided. At one university we found, for example, that the courses were still continued but only for instruction in the evening-school program. At another university, which was joined with six other schools via a television cable, the viewing room, the set, and the program were still available to the students. But, although the school still paid its membership dues in the association, no particular effort was being made to urge students to watch. As one administrator wryly stated, occasionally a student or two would wander into the viewing room, but usually because they could think of no other place to go.

Quite aside from the incentive of seed money or an enthusiastic proponent, innovations may be introduced because of some crisis situation. Rogers (1962) points to the fact that a crisis tends to emphasize the relative advantage of an innovation and affects its rate of adoption. Several schools in our sample were, in fact, confronted by a general crisis in higher education, the campus population explosion, and, for the most part, our information would

140

confirm Miles' observation (1964) that "Sheer size and growth of an [educational] system tend to force adaptive changes and increased concern for innovation" (p. 645). On many larger campuses the increased enrollment is proceeding ahead of the stepped-up building program. This increases the attractiveness of an innovation such as ITV. But as soon as the building program catches up, the need for ITV rapidly diminishes and is frequently abolished. Later, when the upper limit of potential classroom space again lags behind enrollment, the institution may return to the use of the medium. This is a hypothetical case—we did not find all of these factors at any one school—but the factors involved here are important to understanding the institutionalization of an innovation. For example, it would be interesting to determine to what extent these campuses are trying to adapt their classrooms for ITV at a later date by providing closed-circuit television facilities over which programs could be telecast to dormitories and other buildings. Some schools reported that they were making such provisions.

The reasons which universities give for terminating an ITV program are extremely varied. Some appear to be quite superficial, such as the fact that no one on campus was qualified to operate the equipment. In other cases the reasons were more basic. Often we were told that the original need, real or perceived, was no longer present. More buildings had been built; more instructors had been hired; enrollment had been reduced. Other frequent reasons for termination were that the funds which had initiated the program had come to an end or that the enthusiastic faculty proponent or the ITV supporter from administration had left the campus or had lost his enthusiasm. Sometimes our interviewees were completely open in admitting that faculty hostility and perhaps even student resistance had delivered a death blow to the program. Again, all these reasons actually indicate the lack of institutionalization of the innovation.

In a review of Bereday's and Lauwerys' *Communication Media and the School* (1960), Evans (1961) points out that the high rate of failure of audio-visual programs might well be traced

141

to the amount of hardware and effort it requires on the part of a school and its members. Faculty members and administrators in our sample also seemed to be saying again and again, "We really don't want ITV because it takes too much effort." Even if the university had the money to introduce an innovation, its initiation would mean that they would have to learn to do something in a new way —and that, of course, requires effort.

❦ QUALITY EDUCATION ❦

One charge frequently levied against instructional television, teaching machines, and other innovations in communication media is that they water down the quality of education. Hence, we found it quite interesting to explore with our respondents those factors which they felt contribute to quality education. In general, they agreed with the majority of the Metro University faculty: Quality education is achieved in face-to-face confrontation of professors and a small class of students. Some of the smaller colleges in our sample were actually operating on this type of program and justified their higher tuition rates by pointing to the smaller student-faculty ratio. However, the larger state-supported campuses found such a program impossible. Nevertheless, the idea of quality education based on small student-teacher ratios survives even in these large institutions.

At least three schools that we visited were trying to build up within the university two subsystems, each with a different role and different methods. One subsystem offered large enrollment courses which could accommodate up to two thousand or three thousand students, whose education must be limited to the transmission of information. Within this larger system an attempt was also being made to build a small academic community. This second subsystem may be housed in a special part of the campus called "University College," or may be just a so-called honors program, and generally consists of a small but highly select group of honor students, perhaps 500 in number. Again, this program appeared to us

142

to be an ambiguous response to the challenge of innovation. While the move toward providing quality education for at least a small number of students in itself represents an innovation on some campuses, the methods of teaching in these subsystems are far from innovative; as a matter of fact, there frequently is a reversion to the most archaic forms of teaching. Conversely and ironically, the large enrollment system may be forced to use technological innovations or, of necessity, find some new and expedient ways to provide mass education. A most interesting question arises from these observations. If in any teaching-learning system we decide that the best we can do to cope with sheer numbers of students is to shelve our traditional ideas of quality education and simply insure some information gain and acquisition of certain skills, will instructional innovations be more readily accepted? We think so.

Quality education, we were repeatedly told by our respondents, involves more than just transmission of information and training in skills. This extra ingredient, they felt, is present in the more traditional teaching methods, but lacking in ITV and teaching-machine programs. Obviously, then, in the study of acceptance and rejection of innovation in higher education, we must attempt to identify and analyze this extra ingredient. We predict that this will not be an easy task. At least we repeatedly encountered great difficulty in getting our respondents to elaborate on what the factor or factors might be, although this extra ingredient seemed of paramount importance to them. If what most professors expect of their classes at the end of the semester can be judged by looking at their exams, little more than the dissemination of information and training in certain skills can be said to be their goals. Under the circumstances we are led to hypothesize that this educational plus is not clearly defined in the professor's own mind, that in-depth interviews might reveal that he is worshipping something that is rather amorphous and ambiguous. In fact, such a hypothesis provides a not unreasonable explanation of why so much of the resistance to innovation, which appears to threaten this special quality education, is vague in purpose and direction. This resistance may simply be some-

143

thing which traditionally is passed on from one generation of professors to another.

To attack this problem empirically appears to be difficult but not impossible. We might begin by looking systematically at what takes place in the university setting besides simply the transmission of information and the teaching of skills. Sanford (1967), for example, focuses on the development of the personality of the student in his examination of this question. Is it possible that the professor must examine the needs of his students in order to define what he means by this "quality in education" he appears to be seeking? Is it possible that the professor is actually coping with the development of student values and creativity, and confuses this with the more apparent nature of the content which he communicates?

Another focus might be on a determination of professorial goals which are unique to certain disciplines in comparison with those which vary from discipline to discipline. However, whatever the focus, more precise knowledge concerning what professors mean by "quality education" is clearly called for in order to interpret many of our findings.

❧ INNOVATING AND INNOVATION-RESISTING PROFESSOR ❧

Whenever our discussion on the nine campuses turned to the personality factors characteristic of our two prototypes, the innovator and the laggard, the pro-ITV and the anti-ITV professor, a lively and sometimes heated discussion followed, particularly in the faculty groups. We usually reviewed our findings briefly by stating that in our case study we found that those who resisted ITV appeared to be more narrowly restricted in their interests within the university, that they carried larger teaching loads, that they tended to be more resistant to psychological testing, and that they tended to be a little more anxious in general. We pointed out that we found significantly more resistance in certain disciplines, primarily in the humanities rather than in the technological fields. On the other hand, we reported, in our case study the professor who favored ITV tended to extend his interest beyond the university, had broader interests, carried a smaller teaching load, and was often more productive in such non-teaching activities as writing and research.

After presenting these findings, we asked our respondents if those who resisted innovations at their university might be similarly classified; in other words, did our prototypes seem to describe the resisters on their campus? Generally, the responses from both faculty and administrators were confirmatory. However, there were some notable exceptions. As we would have predicted, some of our interviewees were quite disturbed by these dichotomies. Often one of the first questions they raised concerned the validity of generalizations across innovations. They were quick to point out that a faculty member who strongly resists one particular innovation, like ITV, may himself be the innovator for another change. Again predictably, those of our interviewees who were themselves involved in the humanities and perhaps viewed themselves as teachers rather than researchers challenged this whole assumption. Some stated that the humanities are many centuries older than other academic areas and their resources are to be found within the confines of the university itself; therefore, no purpose is served by going outside the system, since all that is needed is contained within the library.

Generally—though this was by no means true in every case—administrators discussed the issues relating to personality and other characteristics of resisters more readily and openly than faculty members, particularly when the discussion turned to specific academic areas from which they expected the greatest amount of resistance to innovations. To a large extent, this reaction may have been the result of our procedure rather than a real difference between the openness of faculty members and administrators. Obviously, the latter were freer to express their opinions since the interview took place within the confines of their private offices, with only the interviewer present. On the other hand, faculty members who were interviewed in groups were quite aware that their colleagues, as well as the investigator, could hear what they were saying. Perhaps, then, it is even more significant that here, too, we obtained considerable confirmation of our hypotheses. One more important factor must be mentioned in this connection. While disciplines commonly included among the humanities were most frequently listed as sources of resistance, other areas were certainly not immune. On some campuses, schools of education and even engineering departments were most resistant to innovation.

We were repeatedly challenged about how to determine the value of an innovation. Some interviewees pointed out that many, if not most, innovations are worthless (for example, ITV). Is a faculty member not justified in resisting an innovation which he considers of little or no use? At times we were accused of equating innovation with progress and implying that all innovations are good. If we agreed with our respondents that not all innovations are equally valuable, they then brought up the difficulty of judging which are and which are not. What objective criteria do we have, they would ask, for measuring the relative merit of an innovation?

Security, our interviewees generally felt, was another important variable in the behavior of a professor towards an innovation. They repeatedly agreed that the younger, less established professor, with the heavier teaching load and probably lower salary, was indeed more likely to resist innovations. One dean, an educator for over 25 years, said: "In my earlier days, young prospective instructors used to come to the school asking for an opportunity to put new ideas in teaching to work. Their main concern was about freedom to institute new programs, new approaches. Today the young instructor, with the ink still wet on his doctor's degree, asks about security, tenure, and retirement benefits. He says very little about introducing new ideas but shows a great concern for 'fitting-in.' Thus, innovations in a university are introduced by the older, more secure faculty member."

That security is a powerful factor in the university is indicated in yet another way. In some cases, even one who is generally innovative may become a resister when his own security is threatened. Security here does not always mean money or tenure; sometimes it involves the defense of one's discipline. We found an interesting example of this at a school which had introduced the core humanities curriculum. The supradepartmental nature of the program brought about strong resistance from professors, not because they saw their jobs threatened but because they feared the consequences of losing their departmental footing.

Many among those whom we interviewed felt that our cosmopolite-localite dimension is highly oversimplified. Surely, they asserted, people do not have to fall into one or the other camp. There must be a middle ground. We assured them that we thought a middle ground does exist and that people may fall at any point along a continuum. Many pointed out again that an individual could be at different points of a continuum at different times, depending on the particular innovation. In other words, a person could be sympathetic to one innovation while resisting another. But even after our respondents had stated all these reservations, they usually agreed that our hypothesis has considerable validity. Faculty members and administrators alike felt that the personality of the professor, his array of interests, and his narrowness or breadth of scope are indeed important areas for further research.

❧ SUMMARY AND DISCUSSION ❧

The information gathered in this phase of our investigation leaves us with little doubt that the findings of our research case history are not only characteristic of the Metro faculty. In other words, respondents from the nine campuses we visited confirmed most of our findings, even if only through our informal interviews. However, many questions remain unanswered and will require additional research. We are now quite aware that many of our terms, such as innovation, cosmopolite, and localite will require further research-based elaboration as we proceed.

Our data clearly emphasized the need for gathering more objective information about the attitudes, beliefs, and values of professors, together with additional subjective evaluations from their students. In this area more definitive knowledge about the meaning of "quality education" should be obtained. We need to find more behavioral items which characterize professors along the cosmopolite-localite continuum. What is their behavior on the campus itself? We can quite reasonably expect—as some of our respondents pointed out to us—that those who fall between the two extremes are of great importance in the innovation process. Our data do not justify, nor do we wish to imply, that being an extreme cosmopolite is necessarily good and being a localite is bad. Without more data we find it difficult to speculate, but perhaps we will find that a prototype who has attributes of both the cosmopolite and the localite will be the ideal professor type, as well as being a decisive force in the innovation process.

These data suggest certain limitations of employing superficial behavior-oriented items in devices designed to differentiate one group from another. While such overt behavioral items as participation in national meetings, professional travel, the extent of teaching experience at other institutions, and the number of subscriptions to professional journals might give some indication of an individual's life style, the psychological factors underlying this behavior or more elaborate reports of behavior might be of even greater importance. As we suggested earlier, a journal subscriber is under no obligation to read the magazines he receives, nor is the conference goer compelled to attend meetings or to listen to the papers presented. Undoubtedly, a person may often give an appearance of mobility which actually comes from nothing more than random or undirected travel. We could come up with a whole series of overt behavior items which might characterize a cosmopolite or localite and find that they are not at all reliable indices. We need, then, a device which will measure more intrinsic and comprehensive reports of behavior. From this we would want to find out not only whether a given group of professors go to conventions but how many meetings they really attend, and—more importantly—as a result of such attendance, what changes occur in their professional activities when they return to the campus. On the other hand, another group of individuals may be scored as localites on an item related to travel when, in fact, their desire to travel is hampered only by budget limitations. Since the factor analysis in our research case history—along with our chi square tests—indicates that these overt behavioral factors are significant, we are led to conclude from our interviews that we must explore these variables with much greater sensitivity and comprehensiveness by building whole clusters of extrinsic and intrinsic items which would contribute to a clearer picture.

For example, professional travel does seem to us to be a most important factor, particularly relating to the cosmopolite-localite hypotheses. The age of the jet plane, the increased number of national and international meetings, and the availability and tremendous impact of communication facilities certainly mean that the professor is no longer dependent only on the library to broaden his scope of knowledge. Through public media, visits to other universities, and attendance at national and international conferences, the whole world becomes, as it were, his library or his laboratory. This raises many interesting questions for research. For example, what happens to the professor for whom opportunity for travel is provided by research grants or university budgets? Does he, as a result of this exposure to the world, question methods and procedures at his own institution? Does he bring back new ideas which may represent the seeds for innovation on his campus?

In a sense, of course, this broadening of horizons is in itself an innovation; although it is one which is both nation-wide and world-wide, it nevertheless has direct effects on the university community. Along with innovations in data processing, data storage and retrieval, and communication, this increased mobility affects an institution regardless of the strength of its resistance. These innovations are in a class by themselves, for individuals and subgroups in our culture are not really free to accept or reject them. The whole university can resist instructional television, but it cannot ignore the fact that students and professors alike watch open-circuit commercial television and are influenced by it. Undoubtedly, these broad cultural innovations forced upon the university system have an effect upon the other innovations that are more voluntary within the university.

In discussions over the years with Marshall McLuhan, the senior author has been particularly interested in his assertions about the restricting effects of operating in what he calls our backward-oriented "print culture." We feel, along with McLuhan in *Understanding Media* (1964), that we are rapidly moving into a culture characterized by the dynamic present constantly stimulated by the instantaneous communication of electronic media. Although society and the university may be slow in breaking away from the restrictions of our "print culture," we believe that it inevitably will be supplanted because of the sheer bombardment of the newer means of communication. Strong indications show already that some areas such as physics, chemistry, and biology are no longer primarily shaped by a print culture in disseminating knowledge, but require a far broader range of immediate experience. Change seemingly, then, does not affect all parts of an institution equally. We would certainly agree that an educational system has many characteristics which can change, while others appear to remain fixed. Furthermore, it appears likely that change within the system does not have an equal impact on all of its members; thus, some members can very well remain unaffected by such an event.

The reader may recall that our factor analysis, reported in Chapter 5, shows that for some professors ITV was in itself an isolated object of concern, while for others it was apparently one of several interrelated objects within the university climate, all of which they reacted to favorably or unfavorably. We were not surprised, then, that some of our respondents at the nine universities, while objecting to ITV, strongly emphasized that they were sympathetic to other changes. Perhaps, one of the first questions we need to study is what do university professors perceive as innovation? We recognize, of course, that what may appear as an innovation to one professor is hardly considered such by another. Furthermore, one member of a university may feel that a particular innovation threatens him while another does not view it in this light at all. So if a person wishes to implement change, he must recognize that an individual's immediate perception of such an innovation depends upon the context of his situation. As a hypothesis this is similar to the relationship of perception to context as stated in the Adaptation Level Theory (Helson, 1947). In the final analysis, successful diffusion of an innovation may depend, then, on the climate within a given university. However, since the so-called climate of reception can easily change in time at a given institution, predicting the future date of an innovation from the present climate of a university is not always possible.

# NINE

1. An attempt to integrate some of the theoretical models in the present literature on innovation.
2. The analysis of a research case history of an innovation, instructional television, in one university.
3. A preliminary examination of how far we might generalize some of the inferences from the research case history to nine other universities.

A number of hypotheses emerging from these efforts appear at various points throughout this book. A brief review of the major variables implicit in these hypotheses, which, we feel, affect the innovation process in higher education, might be helpful now, hopefully as a stimulus to future research.

First of all, the concept of innovation itself might bear further examination. Repeatedly this question presented itself to us: Can we meaningfully speak of innovation as a single variable or does a variety of categories of innovation exist—for example, technical, social, and economic—each itself representing a unique variable? Although we have given evidence to show that some professors have consistent attitudes toward innova-

OVERVIEW: MAJOR VARIABLES AND FUTURE RESEARCH POSSIBILITIES

We have undertaken three approaches to the identification of meaningful psychological variables involved in the process of innovation in the American university—an area of inquiry which we feel has been virtually ignored by behavioral scientists. These approaches consist of the following:

tions in general, we think it quite likely that other professors are very selective about the kind of innovations which they are willing to accept. Secondly, regardless of the nature of an innovation, the degree to which individuals view it as consonant or disconsonant with the existing instructional process will affect its acceptance or rejection. Some of our respondents, for example, saw ITV as a simple extension of their own teaching efforts, while others perceived it as a completely autonomous part of the learning-teaching system, with no relationship to their own classroom teaching.

Somewhat related to this variable are two other characteristics of innovation. The first of these is complexity. To utilize ITV many professors seemed to think that much training, equipment, and general re-evaluation of teaching goals and activities would be required. Furthermore, evidence seems to indicate that if a complex innovation can be broken down into "palatable bits," at least partial acceptance will be more rapidly effected. Thus, ITV appeared to be more acceptable to our respondents if they viewed it as an adjunct to present traditional teaching methods—in other words, that it be adopted only for certain courses or be used in conjunction with small discussion groups, must as traditionally large lecture sections have been used in many universities.

Another variable, the source (external or internal to a system) from which the innovation is introduced appears to have an effect quite independent of the variables cited above. In our investigation, evidence indicates that the degree of acceptance of an innovation by professors may partly depend on whether they viewed the innovation as being instituted or imposed by the university administration or whether they felt that it originated within their own academic departments as a result of their own planning.

Some variables that we noted are related directly to the nature of the innovation-receiving system. Our data lead us to believe that some institutions, more than others, provide a more receptive social climate for the introduction and acceptance of innovations. Such universities may be self-energizing in that they attract a greater number of professors who are receptive to innovation.

153

Conversely, the very nature of such universities may tend to exclude those who seek a social climate more reflective of continuing and traditional university patterns. Furthermore, intentionally or unintentionally, such institutions may have built-in channels for introducing and diffusing new ideas and methods. The university fiscal structure might be one illustration of this variable. Financial and budgeting procedures may tend to perpetuate traditional methods —as is often suggested by those advocating change. However, a system's fiscal structure may provide for experimentation and innovation. Some institutions appear to encourage innovation by rewarding the innovator through either increased rank, salary, and other fringe benefits, or even praise.

In addition to these variables, a number of perhaps more obvious ones exist. They include the size and characteristics of the community surrounding the university and the nature of the institution's major sources of funds.

We suggest that a nation-wide, representative sample of professors, administrators, and students from a cross-section of colleges and universities could provide valuable information about the role of the institution itself in fostering or discouraging innovation. Among other practical and theoretical insights which could emerge from such data would be a comparison of responses from colleges having an unusual history of receptivity to various innovations with those given at colleges known to be more tradition oriented.

One of the strongest single suggestions that emerges from the present report is that extremely far-sighted programs must be a vital part of any attempt to institute innovations within the university. We might propose that techniques of instrumental reinforcement, scheduled with carefully preplanned precision as outlined in such current models of reinforcement theory as those of Ferster and Skinner (1957), might well be projected over a period of several years from the time an innovation is first introduced into a system.

The reversion effect discussed earlier occurs most often where reinforcers are not programmed beyond certain minimum limits. Perhaps, the first task is to determine empirically what the most

154

effective reinforcers for the continuance of an innovation are. In universities, salary increments, promotions, and overt administrative approval as a form of status for the innovator are the most frequently used reinforcers. Are there others of a more subtle nature? If long-range commitment is not secured by programmed schedules of the appropriate and most effective reinforcement, then we can suspect that the innovation will be short-lived from the outset. If innovation is to be more than a game of musical chairs—that is, if genuine innovation is to occur and become institutionalized—long-term programming of continuing reinforcement may have to become an integral part of the innovation-receiving system. Accidental or trial-and-error support for innovations has resulted in occasional short-term adoption. However, significant change seems unlikely to occur in a university—if indeed we wish it—if the present system of diffusion continues.

Finally, we have considered a number of variables concerning the innovator himself. A particularly interesting and timely conception is the cosmopolite-localite dimension since it may be related to the degree of an individual's receptivity to change. Future research focused on exploring this dimension depends largely on the adequacy of the operational definitions for the concepts "cosmopolite" and "localite." Precise definitions are needed to construct the adequate psychological tests required for a meaningful research effort. A complicating aspect of the measurement problem comes from the suggestion of some observers that innovators are in both the cosmopolite and localite groups; however, the innovations which members of each group would support belong in different categories.

Somewhat related to the preceding point is the question concerning the receptivity of the various academic disciplines to innovation. Quite possibly, those who favor ITV are more likely to come from the more applied or practical areas rather than from the more traditional disciplines of the university. We can reasonably assume that the more applied areas (for example, engineering, education, and business administration) are actually more dependent

155

on, and hence more oriented toward, the surrounding community; as a result, professors in these areas might more readily accept certain innovations that are more prominent in their activities outside the university. Other innovations, of course, they might reject. In this case, cosmopolitanism might be the result of direct daily experience, a matter of necessity rather than of choice. However, for those in the more traditional disciplines or the less pragmatic areas, such external contacts might represent an expending of some special effort outside their daily routine.

We think it highly plausible that an individual's position in the university system—for example, his academic rank, which is usually closely related to his job security—bears some relationship to his receptivity to innovation. This, in fact, may represent one of the major keys to understanding the rejection of certain kinds of innovations in the university community. The young faculty member, who is not yet completely integrated into the system, may be more willing to experiment with newer methods, but becomes discouraged when he learns that the system appears to reward conforming rather than innovating behavior. He soon perceives that his future depends on "playing the game," at least until he has a secure "foothold" in the system. On the other hand, the senior faculty member with a secure footing may be less willing to abandon traditional methods in favor of new ones. His behavior has been "shaped" to conform to the system, and his innovative predispositions may have been extinguished.

This discussion of variables, emerging from our research efforts, is by no means intended to be exhaustive. The real impetus to future research in this area will depend, to a large extent, upon placing such variables in a meaningful research context. We hope that our efforts have helped by identifying not only some crucial variables but also by focusing on the importance of the university as a natural research setting. This important institution can make a valuable contribution to the development of experimental and theoretical formulations in innovation, a neglected area of social psychological inquiry.

APPENDIX I

OSGOOD SEMANTIC
DIFFERENTIAL
ITEMS

OSGOOD SEMANTIC DIFFERENTIAL ITEMS

Each of the concepts listed below was followed by identical adjective pairs, each of which was, in turn, separated by a seven-point scale as shown below:

good	____:____:____:____:____:____:____	bad
rough	____:____:____:____:____:____:____	smooth
honest	____:____:____:____:____:____:____	dishonest
passive	____:____:____:____:____:____:____	active
fair	____:____:____:____:____:____:____	unfair
weak	____:____:____:____:____:____:____	strong
fast	____:____:____:____:____:____:____	slow
unpleasant	____:____:____:____:____:____:____	pleasant
hard	____:____:____:____:____:____:____	soft
worthless	____:____:____:____:____:____:____	valuable

Concepts:

1. Metro Festival (student festival held annually)
2. Night students
3. Athletic scholarships
4. Additional tuition increase
5. Higher entrance requirements for Metro University
6. More fringe benefits with smaller salary increases
7. Larger salary increases with fewer additional fringe benefits
8. Metro University becoming a state university
9. Admitting qualified Negroes to Metro University
10. Emphasis on research at Metro University
11. Training in teaching methods for professors
12. Training in teaching methods for prospective professors
13. Lecture method supplemented by small discussion sections for large classes
14. Straight lecture method for large classes
15. Television instruction in introductory courses
16. Straight television instruction for large classes
17. Honors courses consisting only of textbooks and final examinations
18. Correspondence courses
19. Television instruction supplemented by small discussion sections for large classes
20. Television instruction in advanced courses
21. Answering student's questions in large classes
22. Teaching machines
23. Myself as a professor
24. Myself doing publishable research

158

25. Myself conducting an introductory course
26. Myself conducting an advanced course
27. Myself conducting a large class
28. Myself conducting a small class
29. Myself conducting a lecture course
30. Myself conducting a television course

 APPENDIX II

*SUPPLEMENTARY
DATA ON FACTOR
ANALYSIS*

Procedure: Although the procedure for factor analysis was described briefly in Chapters 3 and 5, a more detailed discussion follows.

The decision was made to secure rotations by the quartimax method, which attempts to account for variables in as few factors as possible. Factor analytic programs for 300 variables were not readily available at the time; thus, through the use of a unique method developed by Samuel Pinneau, who served as the statistical coordinator for the present study, four stratified samples of 75 variables each were employed. There were three groups for each of the 30 concepts, based on the evaluative, potency, and activity dimensions—or a total of 90 groupings. The scales of the rational categories were randomly assigned to one of the two new groupings, which yielded two comparable groups in terms of their representation of each concept and of the Osgood dimensions. Because "round-off" errors accumulate at such a rapid rate when more than 100 variables are analyzed by the Centroid Factor Analytic Program, each of these groups of 150 scales was broken down into two 75-item groups by taking the odd-numbered items for one of them and the even-numbered items for the other.

The four separate analyses were run through correlational routines and also the Centroid Factor Analytic Program. The factor loadings were then rotated. Twenty factors were extracted from each study of 75 items. Usually a smaller number would be extracted through the use of some criterion for stopping extractions. Admittedly, many of the 20 factors may be meaningless. A different consideration is encountered, however, from using a stratified sampling of variables and combining the factors obtained from four different samples of variables. A given factor which meets a restrictive criterion in one set of items may not meet the criterion in others. Still, the factor could be meaningful and represented in the other group to a measurable extent. Indeed, a factor which does not meet such arbitrary criteria but which is present in two or three of the item groupings could hardly surface by chance and should, therefore, be regarded as meaningful.

Thus, the criterion employed in the present study regards factors as significant if they appear in both of the analyses. But when the analysis is continued beyond the usual bounds, that is, to 20 factors, it seems unlikely that a meaningful factor in any one of the analyses would be left out if it is present to a measurable extent in one of the four matrices.

Only the factor analytic data based on ITV-related items will be presented in the present report, and of these only the first nine factors within each of the four studies. The tables also consider just the items which correlate with hypothetical dimensions (the factor content) to the extent of .25 or greater. The relatively low value was chosen to prevent excluding any variables which might be at least theoretically significant to the nature of the hypothetical dimension.

Results and discussion: In the following results and discussion, the reader will note that we, a priori, placed "labels" on the various factors which have emerged. We hope that the reader will recognize (as one always must when dealing with results of factor analytic studies) that such labels and broadly related interpretations of factors are basically subjective processes.

As we pointed out in Chapter 5, each of the resulting factors may be conceived as relating to one of two patterns with respect to what ITV meant to the respondents in the present investigation. These two patterns are (1) "pure ITV," or factors showing intra-related concepts within the ITV framework and (2) "ITV with non-ITV," or factors relating ITV concepts to the individual's pre-established attitudes or cognitive structures concerned with the general university climate.

Ten factors which reflect the above patterns are given in detail in the table. In this table, three factors seem to show intra-related ITV attitudes or concepts. One of these "pure-ITV" factors that might be designated as a "Diverse-ITV-Evaluative Factor" appears in all but the fourth study. A second factor that might be designated as a "Diverse-ITV-Potency-Activity Factor" appears in the second study. The third "pure-ITV" factor appears in the fourth study and may be designated "Diverse-ITV-Potency Factor."

FACTOR ANALYSIS

Diverse-ITV-Evaluative Factor

(Study 1 / Factor 2)

	Item	Scale	Loading
1.	Television instruction in introductory course	*Fair*–Unfair	.888
2.	Television instruction in introductory course	*Honest*–Dishonest	.854
3.	Television instruction in introductory course	*Good*–Bad	.763
4.	Television with discussion groups	*Fair*–Unfair	.567
5.	Straight television instruction for large class	Weak–*Strong*	.565
6.	Television in advanced courses	*Fair*–Unfair	.406
7.5	Television with discussion groups	*Fast*–Slow	.398
7.5	Television in advanced courses	*Fast*–Slow	.398
9.	Myself conducting television course	Worthless–*Valuable*	.385
10.	Straight television instruction for large class	Passive–*Active*	.365
11.	Myself conducting television course	*Fair*–Unfair	.348
12.	Correspondence courses	*Honest*–Dishonest	.337
13.	More fringe benefits	*Honest*–Dishonest	.328
14.	Myself conducting television course	*Good*–Bad	.313

(Study 2 / Factor 2)

	Item	Scale	Loading
1.	Television in advanced courses	*Good*–Bad	.824
2.	Television in advanced courses	Worthless–*Valuable*	.822
3.	Television in advanced courses	Weak–*Strong*	.753
4.	Straight television instruction for large class	Worthless–*Valuable*	.390
5.	Straight television instruction for large class	*Fair*–Unfair	.303
6.	Myself conducting television course	Rough–*Smooth*	.282
7.	Straight television instruction for large class	Rough–*Smooth*	.260

(Study 3 / Factor 2)

	Item	Scale	Loading
1.	Television with discussion groups	Worthless–*Valuable*	.832
2.	Television instruction in introductory courses	Worthless–*Valuable*	.825
3.	Television with discussion groups	*Good*–Bad	.810

FACTOR ANALYSIS

Item	Scale	Loading
4. Television instruction in introductory course	Weak–*Strong*	.712
5. Television with discussion groups	Unpleasant–*Pleasant*	.711
6. Television instruction in introductory course	Unpleasant–*Pleasant*	.703
7. Straight television instruction for large class	Unpleasant–*Pleasant*	.611
8. Straight television instruction for large class	*Honest*–Dishonest	.496
9. Television in advanced courses	Unpleasant–*Pleasant*	.452
10. Television in advanced courses	*Honest*–Dishonest	.416
11. Myself conducting television course	Weak–*Strong*	.357
12. Myself conducting television course	*Honest*–Dishonest	.349
13. Correspondence courses	Passive–*Active*	.258
14. Correspondence courses	Unpleasant–*Pleasant*	.251
15. Metro Festival	Passive–*Active*	.250

Teaching-Technique-Activity-Potency Factor

(Study 1 / Factor 9)

Item	Scale	Loading
1. Training in teaching methods for professors	Rough–*Smooth*	.650
2. Training in teaching methods for professors	*Hard*–Soft	−.546
3. Teaching machines	*Hard*–Soft	−.419
4. Additional tuition increase	*Fast*–Slow	−.382
5. Television with discussion groups	Rough–*Smooth*	.372
6.5 Honors courses limited to text and exam	*Fast*–Slow	−.312
6.5 Answering questions in large class	Rough–*Smooth*	.312

Diverse-ITV-Potency-Activity Factor

(Study 2 / Factor 7)

Item	Scale	Loading
1. Television with discussion groups	Weak–*Strong*	.645
2. Straight television instruction for large class	Worthless–*Valuable*	.608
3. Straight television instruction for large class	*Fair*–Unfair	.575
4. Television with discussion groups	*Honest*–Dishonest	.558
5. Television instruction in introductory course	Passive–*Active*	.373
6. Television instruction in introductory course	Rough–*Smooth*	.318

164

FACTOR ANALYSIS

Evaluative-Didactic-Instruction Factor

(Study 2 / Factor 9)

Item	Scale	Loading
1. Straight lecture method	Worthless–*Valuable*	.819
2. Straight lecture method	*Fair*–Unfair	.756
3. Straight lecture method	Unpleasant–*Pleasant*	.492
4. Straight television instruction for large class	Worthless–*Valuable*	.304
5. Straight television instruction for large class	*Fair*–Unfair	.280

Calculating-Realistic-Potency Factor

(Study 3 / Factor 4)

Item	Scale	Loading
1. Emphasis on research	*Hard*–Soft	.672
2. Myself conducting television course	*Hard*–Soft	.640
3. Myself conducting large class	*Hard*–Soft	.618
4. Myself publishing research	*Hard*–Soft	.590
5. Higher entrance requirements	*Hard*–Soft	.553
6. Metro Festival	*Hard*–Soft	.466
7. Honors courses of text and exam	Rough–*Smooth*	−.449
8. Myself conducting television course	*Honest*–Dishonest	.391
9. Myself conducting an introductory course	*Fast*–Slow	.340
10. Admitting qualified Negroes	Rough–*Smooth*	−.314
11. Night students	*Fair*–Unfair	.304
12. Becoming a state university	Rough–*Smooth*	−.268
13. Larger salary increases	*Fast*–Slow	.255
14. Myself conducting advanced course	*Honest*–Dishonest	.235

Self-Evaluative Factor

(Study 3 / Factor 8)

Item	Scale	Loading
1. Myself conducting large class	*Honest*–Dishonest	.639
2. Myself conducting advanced course	*Honest*–Dishonest	.582
3. Training in methods for prospective professors	*Honest*–Dishonest	.387
4. Emphasis of research	*Honest*–Dishonest	.347
5. Myself conducting television course	*Honest*–Dishonest	.318

Diverse-ITV-Potency Factor

(Study 4 / Factor 4)

1.	Television instruction in introductory course	*Hard*–Soft	.761
2.	Straight television instruction for large class	*Hard*–Soft	.754
3.	Television in advanced courses	*Hard*–Soft	.651
4.	Television with discussion groups	*Hard*–Soft	.568
5.	Training in methods for prospective professors	*Hard*–Soft	.363
6.	Television in advanced courses	Passive–*Active*	.253

The "Diverse-ITV-Evaluative Factor" shows the intrarelationship of evaluative attitudes of ITV with its application to (1) introductory courses; (2) discussion groups; (3) advanced courses; (4) large courses; and (5) self-evaluations as ITV professors. Also appearing in this factor is an apparent relationship of ITV to correspondence courses. We might note here that the extreme pro- and anti-ITV groups also responded to the concept of "Correspondence courses" in a manner similar to their responses to ITV concepts, that is, the pro-ITV group gave a significantly higher evaluation to "Correspondence courses" than did the anti-ITV group. (See discussion of pro-ITV versus anti-ITV group data in Chapter 6.) Although the factor loading on the "Correspondence-courses" item never exceeded .337, the fact that it occurred three times lends some validity to the statement of a relationship of faculty attitudes toward such courses and their attitude toward ITV. Of the 36 items loading on this factor in three different studies, 25 are from the Osgood Evaluative Scales.

Another factor which illuminates some intrarelatedness of ITV items is the "Diverse-ITV-Potency-Activity Factor." This factor appears as the seventh factor in Study 2. The most heavily loaded item in this factor is "TV with discussion groups—Strong" (.645). Half the items appearing in this factor are from either Osgood Activity or Potency Scales. From data on this factor we might hypothesize that ITV attitudes show an activity-potency intrarelationship among the concepts of ITV as applied to (1) discussion groups, (2) large classes, and (3) introductory courses. In general, we might say that this factor reflects an activity-potency facet concerning the nature of many of the items included in the "Diverse-ITV-Evaluative Factor."

The final factor to be discussed here concerning intrarelationships of concepts within the ITV framework is the "Diverse-ITV-Potency Factor," which appears as the fourth of Study 4. All but one of the six items loading on this factor are from the Osgood Potency Scale, "hard-soft." The single exception is the least heavily loaded item, "ITV in Advanced Courses—Active." Again, intrarelationships occur between ITV with (1) discussion groups, (2) TV for large classes, (3) TV for introductory courses, (4) TV with discussion groups, and (5) TV in advanced courses. A relationship of ITV to "Training in teaching methods for prospective professors" also appears in this factor.

Conceptualizations of aspects of ITV and attitudes toward them appear related to non-ITV concepts and attitudes in four factors. The first, which is designated as a "Didactic-Instruction-Evaluative Factor," appears as the ninth factor in Study 2. The relationship between "Straight lecture method" and "Straight TV for large classes" might reflect less concern with ITV as such, but rather it indicates a limited didactic approach to teaching in general. All five items loading on this factor are from the Osgood Evaluative Scales.

In the factor "Teaching Technique-Activity-Potency Factor," relationships of ITV to other teaching methods are shown. The only ITV item which appears within this factor is "TV with discussion groups." It seems to be related to the concepts "Training in teaching methods for professors," "Teaching machines," "Answering questions in large classes," "Honors courses," and "Additional tuition increase." With the exception of the item about "Additional tuition," we might conceive of this factor as indicating an integration of ITV conceptualizations with an existing cognitive structure. Such a structure might reflect a preoccupation with a variety of teaching methods.

167

The third factor related to ITV with non-ITV attitudes and conceptualizations appears in the third study and is designated a "Self-Evaluative Factor." Among the items appearing in this factor ("honest-dishonest" Osgood Evaluative Scale) are three "myself" items, including "Myself conducting a TV course." Apparently related to these "myself" evaluations are "Training in teaching methods for prospective professors" and "Emphasis on research." Again, we have here an instance of ITV's being integrated into an already existing focus of concern. In this instance, the cognitive structure might be regarded as a concern with the professor's self-image and "doing the right thing" in terms of what is expected of him in the university climate.

All the items in the above "Self-Evaluative Factor" also appear in the third factor, which we labeled as a "Calculating Real-istic-Potency Factor." This factor seems to reflect a relationship of its included items with those appearing loaded on the "Self-Evaluative Factor." Whereas in the "Self-Evaluative Factor" the professor seems to display a subjective concern with himself and the appropriateness of his behavior, here he is concerned with his competence to assess concrete realities objectively. Among the wide range of interrelated concepts appearing in this factor are "Emphasis on research"; "Myself conducting TV introductory and advanced courses"; "Higher entrance requirements"; "Myself doing publishable research"; and "Metro University becoming a state university." Of the 14 items loaded on this factor, 9 are from the Osgood Potency Scales. Here we see a strong tendency to view things as they "really" are with a skeptical, "no-nonsense" approach.

APPENDIX III

*COMPARISONS
BETWEEN
PROFESSORS'
ATTITUDES
TOWARD ITV
IN THE PRESENT
STUDY AND FOUR
PREVIOUS
UNIVERSITY
STUDIES*

CODE:

Abbreviation	Study	Television Method Employed
Met.	Metro University	Video-tape and studio playback only
Mi.	Miami University	Closed-circuit television
Ore.	Oregon State system of higher education	Interinstitutional (four participating schools)
P-1	Pennsylvania State University, Project No. 1	Closed-circuit television
P-2	Pennsylvania State University, Project No. 2	Closed-circuit television

CATEGORIES

Study[1]

GF = General faculty

TEI = Television-Experienced Instructor

	Met.	Mi.	Ore.	P-1	P-2
ECONOMIC FACTORS					
FAVORABLE					
Economy of staff and facilities: ITV saves time, expense, or space; productivity of faculty members per hour of class instruction can be increased; ITV offers more efficient use of visual aids and demonstrations; television instructors can cover more material; lectures can be re-used (caution re: royalty arrangements); ITV should make it practical for faculty members to have some assistance in teaching; working relationships between television and audio-visual department staffs are satisfactory; also ITV can reduce teacher shortage.	GF TEI	GF TEI	GF	GF	GF
Reaches more students: With ITV, instructor can teach greater number of students; thus it could be an answer to increased enrollment.	GF TEI	GF TEI	GF		GF

171

[1] *Experimental Study in Instructional Procedures,* Oxford, Ohio: Miami University, 1960; *Instructional Television Research Report One and Two: An Investigation of Closed-Circuit Television for Teaching University Courses,* University Park, Pa.: The Pennsylvania State University, 1958; *Inter-Institutional Teaching by Television,* Portland, Oregon: Oregon State System of Higher Education, Report No. 1, 1957–1959.

ECONOMIC FACTORS (Continued)

UNFAVORABLE

	Met.	Mi.	Ore.	P-1	P-2
Not economical: No manpower is saved considering the amount of auxiliary help necessary; no saving in time with ITV; ITV requires more preparation; expensive in terms of original equipment cost; use of ITV should be deferred until it becomes absolutely necessary; also, ITV requires special training.	GF TEI		GF	TEI	
Will partially absorb millions of dollars for education under the guise of public relations.	GF				

INSTRUCTOR FACTORS

FAVORABLE

	Met.	Mi.	Ore.	P-1	P-2
Rewarding: Some respond favorable to having themselves and their work widely observed; some feel greater sense of personal satisfaction; some think ITV offers a challenge.	GF	TEI		GF TEI	GF

UNFAVORABLE

	Met.	Mi.	Ore.	P-1	P-2
Fears of inadequacy: Some feel self-conscious; some are concerned about the high degree of visibility of each television teacher.	TEI	TEI	GF		GF
Favorable experience with teaching large classes causes some to oppose ITV.					GF
Preparation time and strain factor: ITV results in increased or too much preparations; extra training is necessary; teaching before camera increases stress on instructor already under strain; the mechanics of the	GF TEI	GF TEI	TEI	GF TEI	GF

172

ITV situation are disturbing; to make an error on television can be a traumatic experience; no objections to ITV if teaching load were lighter; restriction in use of blackboard requires changing of instructors' habits.

Restrictions and handicaps: Freedom of expression is limited; psychological distance between instructor and student is severe handicap; loss of reward resulting from teacher-student relationship in traditional teaching situation; ITV is not rewarding for the teacher.

Role and Status: Staff member has inferior role as section leader; status of professor is jeopardized; teacher's personality is lost; instructor is dehumanized by ITV.

INSTRUCTOR-ADMINISTRATION FACTORS
FAVORABLE

None

INSTRUCTOR-ADMINISTRATION FACTORS
UNFAVORABLE

Administrative problems: Television instruction involves too many administrative duties; the ITV program was launched with insufficient prior study; there are too many scheduling problems; it is impossible to discover who has talent for television instruction; departmental assistance and full administrative support are not assured; administration takes attitude that ITV is cure-all; there is inadequate time for preparation; ITV will lead to an increase in teaching load.

173

GF TEI	GF	GF
GF TEI	GF	GF TEI
	GF	GF
GF	GF	GF

INSTRUCTOR-ADMINISTRATION FACTORS (Continued)

	Met.	Mi.	Ore.	P-1	P-2
Faculty: ITV limits number of qualified instructors; could lead to not enough instructors being trained; faculty will develop a "star system"; professional rivalry will develop between non-ITV and ITV faculty.	TEI			GF	
Threat to job security: ITV will lead to large-scale unemployment; to be viewed by public at-large represents a threat to the instructor; ITV will result in the loss of good faculty members; there must be some assurance that the instructor will not be replaced by television teaching.	GF TEI			GF	

INSTRUCTOR-STUDENT FACTORS

FAVORABLE

	Met.	Mi.	Ore.	P-1	P-2
ITV promotes student interest.			GF		

UNFAVORABLE

	Met.	Mi.	Ore.	P-1	P-2
Impersonal: Television lacks interpersonal relationships; student participation is limited; there is less opportunity for questions; student cannot challenge instructor; student identity is lost; lack of contact with students results in absence of stimulation for instructor.	GF TEI	GF TEI	GF TEI	GF TEI	GF
No feedback: Teaching effectiveness cannot be judged; pace of presentation is difficult to determine; barriers are raised between instructor and student.	GF	GF TEI	GF TEI	GF	GF
Students: ITV produces discipline problems; opposition and resentment of television develops; students are seriously inhibited in the room from which a closed-circuit telecast originates.	GF			TEI	GF

174

INTANGIBLE FACTORS

FAVORABLE

None

UNFAVORABLE

Loss of full influence of instruction: Ability to teach students to reason and communicate is inferior; students accept a "lecture authority"; students' ability to think critically is difficult to develop; ITV instruction results in less overall growth and development; conventional teaching has ingredients difficult to measure, which are nonetheless valuable; a "full college education" and the "feel" of a subject cannot be presented over ITV.

GF   TEI   GF   TEI   GF

175

LEARNING FACTORS

FAVORABLE

Good effects on learning: Fewer distractions result from ITV, which can be viewed at home; basic concepts can be learned as well as in conventional classroom instruction; average grades and results are as good as or better than those in the classroom situation; students prefer ITV; students are given more responsibility; ITV may promote standardization of course content.

GF   TEI   GF   GF

LEARNING FACTORS (Continued)

	Met.	Mi.	Ore.	P-1	P-2
UNFAVORABLE					
Bad effects on learning: ITV creates bad learning environment; it may promote automation and standardization; television commercializes and weakens education; it will produce mass mediocrity; learning by television is non-permanent; social aspect of the learning situation is lost; passive absorption or pouring in information results; ITV is bad for introductory courses; it is boring; student attitude toward ITV is poor; misinterpretation of what is being said results because of insufficient background; ITV teaches facts rather than concepts; controversial viewpoints cannot be presented; individual attention to student is lacking.	GF TEI	GF TEI	GF	GF	GF

METHOD AND MATERIAL

	Met.	Mi.	Ore.	P-1	P-2
FAVORABLE					
Better teacher preparation and organization: ITV avoids duplication and gives time for restructuring (if time is provided for this); develops new techniques in teaching; makes possible comparison of different classroom procedures; provides for the possibility of team teaching; reduces reports and papers; two-way communication system could provide opportunity for students' questions; preparation and quality of lectures improves; ITV allows less abstraction.	TEI		GF TEI	GF	GF

EASIER TO TEACH

	Met.	Mi.	Ore.	P-1	P-2
Enriches and improves instruction: ITV is a good supplement and visual aid; outstanding lecturers can be made available to all; ITV	GF TEI	GF TEI	GF	GF	GF

176

offers advantages of demonstrations, panels, interviews, etc.; it is a teaching aid; television offers broader and more orderly presentation of material; it spreads benefits of staff and equipment among institutions; ITV offers advantages of "front-row seating."

UNFAVORABLE

Difficult to teach by television: Even if the overall physical arrangement were acceptable, there are problems with lapel microphone, cord, lights; monitor receiver is sometimes of little use; pick-up microphone for students in television-originating room is frequently unsatisfactory; trial demonstrations are put on without preplanning, resulting in unsatisfactory presentations. — TEI

Inadequate: ITV makes grading difficult (objective-test scores are not adequate); teaching cannot be adapted to individual differences; ITV cannot replace classroom lectures; a good teacher in a small class is better than ITV. — GF, TEI; GF; GF

Limits teaching techniques: ITV fails to motivate students; reduces flexibility of method; emphasizes acting not teaching; television is no better than a textbook; sound tape would be as good as ITV. — TEI; GF

QUALITY

FAVORABLE

Quality of education: ITV raises the standard of introductory courses; high-quality lectures could be used; television improves level of instruc- — TEI; GF, TEI; GF; GF

177

QUALITY (*Continued*)

FAVORABLE (Continued)

tion; exposes more students to better teachers; high quality of instruction; ITV broadens the viewpoints of institutions; an instructor can influence more students, and at the same time he can work with exceptional students individually; ITV raises standards of teaching; ITV can make a contribution to higher education.

UNFAVORABLE

	Met.	Mi.	Ore.	P-1	P-2
Damages quality of higher education: ITV cheapens or lowers quality of education; lowers standards of teaching; lowers level of instruction.	GF TEI		GF		GF

MISCELLANEOUS CURRICULUM EVALUATIONS

FAVORABLE

None

UNFAVORABLE

	Met.	Mi.	Ore.	P-1	P-2
Student inattentiveness: Student relaxes too much.	GF	GF	GF		GF
ITV requires a different student body (one with more initiative and "digging-out" ability).	GF				

178

TYPE OF COURSE

FAVORABLE

Courses (specific): ITV has excellent possibilities for telecasting expensive experiments in the physical sciences; lower-division teaching load could be reduced with ITV.

   GF TEI | GF

Good idea for lecture courses: ITV eliminates large classes; gives more intimate tone; television offers freedom from monotony; it can be a time saver in teaching multiple-section courses; ITV could be useful in extending information; it can overcome barriers insurmountable in large classrooms.

   GF | GF | GF

UNFAVORABLE

Not suited to all courses: Labs or workshops cannot be covered on television; discussion or lab cannot be related to lecture; lack of color in television presentation is a serious limitation for chemistry and art; students cannot examine demonstrations more closely after class; students see only pictures, not actuality; blackboard vision is limited; library and other assignments are difficult to supervise.

   GF TEI | TEI | GF TEI | GF TEI | GF

PROFESSIONAL FACTORS

FAVORABLE

Aids exchanges of teaching techniques and ideas: Television offers cross-fertilization in developing new ideas in a field; it provides less cumber-

   GF | GF | GF

PROFESSIONAL FACTORS (*Continued*)

FAVORABLE (*Continued*)

	Met.	Mi.	Ore.	P-1	P-2
some means of communication than the scholarly journals; television is an ideal way to spread teaching techniques and ideas to other teachers; ITV represents a new means for providing teacher training; instructors should have training in television teaching.					
Instructors are freed to engage in activities related to personal-professional development: ITV eases teacher load by making time-saving, multiple-section teaching possible, thus providing more time for research.	TEI		GF	GF TEI	

UNFAVORABLE

	Met.	Mi.	Ore.	P-1	P-2
Lack of intellectual atmosphere: ITV instruction lacks dignity; it is a cheap method of instruction; "sanctity" of the classroom is abridged.	TEI		GF		
Research: Information about research is inadequate; there is no need for teachers to carry out research.	TEI		GF		

MISCELLANEOUS FACTORS

FAVORABLE

	Met.	Mi.	Ore.	P-1	P-2
Good media: ITV offers good education communication; creates good public relations and publicity; offers levels of instruction ranging from public-information programs to undergraduate work; television is a	GF TEI		GF		GF

	GF	TEI
medium for getting knowledge universally distributed; it promotes academic interest among general public.		
Unlimited audience: ITV widens course opportunities for students; reduces relative isolation on campuses; television is well suited for adult education; it brings education to those unable to attend college; ITV has infinite possibilities; it may well be the wave of the future.	GF	TEI
Political: ITV will meet Communist challenge to our technology.	GF	

UNFAVORABLE

	GF	TEI
Questionable usefulness: ITV is acceptable as experiment but does not warrant operational use; it is a mechanical big brother; it has to be a failure because it is a machine.	GF	
Problems to education: ITV diverts attention from important problems in education; there is a danger that it may become a permanent fixture; ITV is the invention of the devil; it is of little use except in rare cases.	GF	
Political: ITV is dangerous as a potential propaganda weapon.	GF	

181

BIBLIOGRAPHY

ADORNO, T. W., E. FRENKEL-BRUNSWIK, D. J. LEVINSON, and R. N. SANFORD. *The Authoritarian Personality.* New York: Harper, 1950.

ASCH, S. E. *Social Psychology.* Englewood Cliffs, N. J.: Prentice-Hall, 1952.

BARNETT, H. G. *Innovation: the Basis of Cultural Change.* New York: McGraw Hill, 1953.

BEREDAY, G. Z. F., and J. A. LAUWERYS (eds.). *Communication Media and the School. Yearbook Education.* Tarrytown-on-Hudson, N. Y.: World, 1960.

BERELSON, B. "Content Analysis" in G. Lindzey (ed.), *Handbook of Social Psychology.* Reading, Mass.: Addison-Wesley, 1954, Vol. 1, 488–522.

BOWEN, R. O. (ed.). *The New Professors.* New York: Holt, 1960.

CAPLOW, T., and R. J. MCGEE. *The Academic Marketplace.* New York: Basic Books, 1958.

CARTER, C. F., and B. R. WILLIAMS. *Industry and Technical Progress: Factors Governing Speed of Application of Science.* London: Oxford University Press, 1957.

CLEE, J. E., and J. B. RESWICK. "Collaboration in Teaching and Learning: An Experimental Course for Engineering Students" in M. B. Miles (ed.), *Innovation in Education.* New York: Bureau of Publications, Teachers College, Columbia University, 1964, Chapter 3, 79–96.

EURICH, A. C. "The Commitment to Experiment and Innovation in College Teaching." *The Educational Record,* 1964, *45,* No. 1, 49.

EVANS, R. I. "Personal Values as Factors in Anti-Semitism." *Journal of Abnormal and Social Psychology,* 1952, *47,* 749–756.

———. "Review of G. Z. Bereday's and J. A. Lauwery's Communication Media and the School." *Teachers' College Record,* 1961, *63,* No. 1, 80–82.

———. *Students' Attitudes Toward Their Instructors.* Unpublished, 1962.

———. *Conversations with Carl Jung and Reactions from Ernest Jones.* New York: Van Nostrand, 1964.

———. *Dialogue with Erich Fromm.* New York: Harper & Row, 1966. (a)

———. "A New Interdisciplinary Dimension in Graduate Psychological Research Training: Dentistry." *American Psychologist,* 1966, *21,* No. 22, 167–172. (b)

EVANS, R. I., R. G. SMITH, and W. K. COLVILLE. *The University Faculty and Educational Television: Hostility, Resistance, and Change.* Houston: University of Houston, 1962.

——— ——— ———. "The University Faculty and Educational Television: Hostility, Resistance, and Change [modified version]" in J. W. Brown and J. W. Thorton, Jr. (eds.), *New Media in Higher Education.* Washington, D.C.: Association for Higher Education, 1963, 53–55.

EVANS, R. I., B. A. WIELAND, and C. W. MOORE. "The Effect of Experience in Telecourses on Attitudes toward Instruction by Television and Impact of a Controversial Television Program." *Journal of Applied Psychology,* 1961, *45,* No. 1, 11–15.

FERSTER, C. B., and B. F. SKINNER. *Schedules of Reinforcement.* New York: Appleton-Century, 1957.

FESTINGER, L. *A Theory of Cognitive Dissonance.* Evanston, Ill.: Row, Peterson, 1957.

FESTINGER, L., and E. ARONSON. "The Arousal and Reduction of Dissonance in Social Contexts" in D. Cartwright and A. Zander (eds.), *Group Dynamics.* Evanston, Ill.: Row, Peterson, 1960, 214–231.

FESTINGER, L., and J. M. CARLSMITH. "Cognitive Consequences of Forced Compliance." *Journal of Abnormal and Social Psychology,* 1959, *58,* 203–210.

FREEDMAN, M. B. *The College Experience.* San Francisco: Jossey-Bass, 1967.

GAMSON, W. A., and C. G. LIMBERG. *An Analytic Summary of Fluoridation Research: With an Annotated Bibliography.* Boston: Harvard School of Public Health, 1960. (Mimeograph.)

HEIDER, F. "Attitudes and Cognitive Organization." *Journal of Psychology,* 1946, *21,* 107–112.

HEIST, PAUL A. (ed.). *Education for Creativity.* San Francisco: Jossey-Bass, 1968. (In press.)

HELSON, H. "Adaptation-Level as Frame of Reference for Prediction of Psychophysical Data." *American Journal of Psychology,* 1947, *60,* 1–29.

HINCKLEY, E. D., and D. RETHLINGSHAFER. "Value Judgments of

Heights of Men by College Students." *Journal of Psychology,* 1951, *31,* 257–262.

JACOB, P. E. *Changing Values in College.* New York: Harper & Row, 1957.

JENKINS, J., and W. A. RUSSELL. "An Atlas of Semantic Profiles for 360 Words." *American Journal of Psychology,* 1958, *71,* 688–694.

KATZ, E. "The Social Itinerary of Technical Change: Two Studies on the Diffusion of Innovation." *Human Organization,* 1961, *20,* 70–82.

KATZ, E., and M. L. LEVIN. "Traditions of Research on the Diffusion of Innovation." Paper presented at meeting of The American Sociological Association in Chicago, 1959.

KRECH, D., and R. S. CRUTCHFIELD. *Theory and Problems of Social Psychology.* New York: McGraw-Hill, 1948.

KRECH, D., R. S. CRUTCHFIELD, and E. L. BALLACHEY. *Individual in Society.* New York: McGraw-Hill, 1962.

KUMATA, H. "New Media-Research Findings in the U.S.A." in G. Z. F. Bereday and D. Lauwerys (eds.), *Communication Media and the School. Yearbook Education.* Tarrytown-on-Hudson, N. Y.: World, 1960, 231–241.

LAZARSFELD, P. F., and W. THIELENS. *The Academic Mind.* Glencoe, Ill.: Free Press, 1958.

MACCOBY, E. E., and N. MACCOBY. "The Interview: A Tool of Social Science" in G. Lindzey (ed.), *Handbook of Social Psychology.* Reading, Mass.: Addison-Wesley, 1954, Vol. 1, 449–487.

MCKEACHIE, W. J. "Procedures and Techniques of Teaching: A Survey of Experimental Studies" in N. Sanford (ed.), *The American College.* New York: Wiley, 1962, 312–364.

MCLUHAN, H. M. *Understanding Media: The Extensions of Man.* New York: McGraw-Hill, 1964. (First edition.)

MARKS, E. S. "Skin Color Judgments of Negro College Students." *Journal of Abnormal and Social Psychology,* 1943, *38,* 269–376.

MILES, M. B. (ed.). *Innovation in Education.* New York: Bureau of Publications, Teachers College, Columbia University, 1964.

MILLER, G. *The Adoption of Inoculation for Smallpox in England and France.* Philadelphia: University of Pennsylvania Press, 1957.

MORT, P. "Studies in Educational Innovation from the Institute of Administrative Research: An Overview" in M. B. Miles (ed.), *Innovation in Education*. New York: Bureau of Publications, Teachers College, Columbia University, 1964, Chapter 13, 317–329.

NEWCOMB, T. "An Approach to the Study of Communicative Acts." *Psychological Review*, 1953, *60*, 393–404.

OSGOOD, C. E., G. J. SUCI, and P. H. TANNENBAUM. *The Measurement of Meaning*. Urbana: University of Illinois Press, 1957.

OSGOOD, C. E., and P. H. TANNENBAUM. "The Principle Congruity in the Prediction of Attitude Change." *Psychological Review*, 1955, *62*, 42–55.

PHILIP, B. R. "The Effect of General and Specific Labelling on Judgmental Scales." *Canadian Journal of Psychology*, 1951, *5*, 18–28.

PROSHANSKY, H. M., and R. I. EVANS. "American Political Extremism in the 1960's." *Journal of Social Issues*, 1963, *19*, No. 2, 86–106.

ROGERS, E. M. *Diffusion of Innovation*. New York: Free Press, 1962.

ROKEACH, M. (ed.). *The Open and Closed Mind*. New York: Basic Books, 1960.

ROKEACH, M., P. W. SMITH, and R. I. EVANS. "Two Kinds of Prejudice or One?" in M. Rokeach (ed.), *The Open and Closed Mind*. New York: Basic Books, 1960, 132–168.

ROSS, D. H. (ed.). *Administration for Adaptability*. New York: Metropolitan School Study Council, 1958.

RUSSELL, J. D. "Faculty Satisfactions and Dissatisfactions." *Journal of Experimental Education, 31,* No. 2, 1962, 135–139.

SANFORD, N. *Where Colleges Fail*. San Francisco: Jossey-Bass, 1967.

——— (ed.). *The American College*. New York: Wiley, 1962.

———. "Will Psychologists Study Human Problems?" *American Psychologist*, 1965, *20*, No. 3, 192–202.

SHERIF, M. "A Study of Some Social Factors in Perception." *Archives of Psychology*, 1935, Whole No. 187.

SHERIF, M., O. J. HARVEY, B. J. WHITE, W. R. HOOD, and C. SHERIF. *Intergroup Conflict and Cooperation: The Robbers Cave Experiment*. Norman, Okla.: University Book Exchange, 1961.

SIEGEL, S. *Nonparametric Methods for the Behavioral Sciences*. New York: McGraw-Hill, 1956.

SNOW, C. P. "Miasma, Darkness, and Torpidity." *New Statesman*, 1961, *42*, No. 1587, 186.

187

TARDE, G. *The Laws of Imitation.* (Translated by E. C. Parsons.) New York: Holt, 1903.

University of California, Academic Senate Berkeley Division. "Preliminary Report of the Select Committee on Education." May 24, 1965. (Mimeograph.)

WATSON, G. "Utopia and Rebellion: The New College Experiment" in M. B. Miles (ed.), *Innovation in Education.* New York: Bureau of Publications, Teachers College, Columbia University, 1964, Chapter 4, 97–116.

WEBER, M. *From Max Weber: Essays in Sociology.* (Translated by H. Gerth and C. W. Mills.) New York: Free Press, 1958.

WILLIAMS, G. *Some of My Best Friends Are Professors.* New York: Abelard–Schuman, 1958.

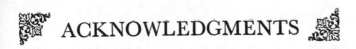

ACKNOWLEDGMENTS

Resistance to Innovation in Higher Education explores various facets of human behavior in a real-life setting, and an unusual effort was necessary to place it in a proper theoretical and research perspective. Many logistical problems have to be solved when television production and personal interviews are carried out with a group that is usually inexperienced in these areas.

Helping us in the research for this book were a number of psychology graduate students. We are greatly indebted to Ronald Smith for his invaluable assistance in analyzing data and compiling and describing results in a preliminary report, of which he was a joint author. We also appreciate the assistance of Mary Ellen Williams, Monna W. Ramsey, Chester May, Noble Enete, and Joseph Fuller. Freelance-writer William Colville, a joint author of the preliminary report, did an outstanding job in helping to coordinate the research presented here.

Many colleagues on the psychology-department faculty must also be cited for their contributions. We thank Daniel E. Sheer and Laurence S. McGaughran for their personal interviews with the faculty population. Samuel Pinneau of San Fernando State College was not only of great assistance in such interviews but made the crucial contribution of designing and implementing the unique factor analysis of the data which emerged from one aspect of this study.

We are indebted to Charles Osgood of the University of Illinois for his invaluable suggestions on the use of the Osgood Semantic Differential in our research case history. The late Carl Hovland of Yale University provided invaluable assistance, suggestions, and ideas in his discussions with us during the beginning stages of the investigation.

The difficult job of coordinating the television-production aspects of the investigation was ably handled by the late Raymond T. Yelkin. Film production in the study was under the supervision of James Bauer. A number of secretaries provided expert assistance. Peggy D. Leppmann completed the final draft of this manuscript. Betsy G. Gandy did an excellent job in completing the preliminary report. The services of Ellen Roberson and Avis Merryfield helped facilitate our work at several crucial points. At the beginning stages of the project, Miss Joyce Brady was of great assistance.

John W. Meaney of Notre Dame University played a critical role in assisting in the development of our research case history.

We wish also to express our appreciation to our faculty consultants at the nine universities discussed in Chapter 9. David Berlo, Richard Bugelski, Robert Hamblin, Shepard Insel, Kenneth Kramer, Cyrus LaGrone, Jack Matthews, Alvin North, and Harold Yuker did an exceptional job of arranging our visits and scheduling the appropriate interviews.

Finally, we greatly appreciate the support of the United States Office of Education in the form of a research grant (#741015) and a contract (#OE-4-16-028) awarded the University of Houston and the Houston Research Institute respectively, with the senior author of this study serving as principal investigator. Without this support we could not have written this book. We are especially grateful to Mr. Thomas Clemens and Mrs. Gertrude Broderick, staff members of the United States Office of Education, for their interest and encouragement.

Richard I. Evans
Peter K. Leppmann

INDEX

76129

76129